LIZZIE RUMMEL

Baroness of the Canadian Rockies

D0943253

Lizzie and Mt. Assiniboine, 1938.

LIZZIE RUMMEL
Baroness of the Canadian Rockies

Ruth Oltmann

Ribbon Creek Publishing Company,
Box 32, Exshaw, Alberta, Canada T0L 2C0

To Lizzie's many friends, but especially to Janey.

*All photographs courtesy of Jane Fisher
unless otherwise indicated.
Jacket design and maps by Brian Patton
Front cover photo by Jim Davies
Back cover photo by Barbara Snyder*

ISBN 0-88925-515-6
Printed and bound in Canada by
Friesen Printers
a Division of D. W. Friesen & Sons Ltd.
Altona, Manitoba, R0G 0B0
Canada

"Books are written by people who have something to say."

Lizzie — 1975

". . . . what she has done will also be told, in memory of her."

Matthew 26:13

ACKNOWLEDGEMENTS

Lizzie had a wonderful host of friends who have been very helpful and who have added much to this story. I will be forever indebted to them for their kindness. In granting me an interview, I would like to thank Timothy Auger, James Bagley, the late James Boyce and Dorothy Boyce, James Deegan, Myrna (Collins) Frank, Lloyd (Kiwi) Gallagher, Dr. J. S. (Smitty) Gardner, Laura Gardner, Jean Gill, Muriel Gratz, Aileen Harmon, the late Charles Hunter, Kenneth and Bridget Jones, Eileen Langille, Joseph Plaskett, Peter Vallance, Jean Walls and James and Deirdre Willer.

I am also indebted to Fr. Peter DeBrul who kindly wrote from Bethlehem, Israel, Catharine McDowell who wrote from Dundrennan, Scotland, Erling Strom who wrote from Oslo, Norway, and Janette Manry who has encouraged me and not lost interest in the project while in Indonesia.

I especially thank E.J. (Ted) Hart, head archivist and Jon Whyte, both of the Archives of the Canadian Rockies, Banff, and their very amiable staff for their many hours of help. I am particularly grateful to Dr. J. S. Gardner and Dr. Gordon W. Hodgson for their wonderful encouragement and Dr. Floyd Snyder for critiquing the manuscript and giving me creative ideas.

I also thank Jane Fisher for the many hours of conversation in which she related the stories of she and her sisters' lives in Europe and on the ranch. Without her help I could never have told the story.

I thank Lizzie too — for being herself and for the years in which I knew and loved her. Lizzie's life has something to say to us all, but especially her courage, kindness and adventuresome spirit have said something to me which I will carry with me forever. May her spirit live on to inspire us all.

R.O.

Contents

CHAPTER I

An Unusual Woman

"I DON'T WANT ANY ARGUMENT."

"What do you mean?"

"No arguments please."

"Alright. What's the matter?"

"I'm going to have a picnic on Og Pass and I'm inviting you and you're to come, and I'm inviting Eileen Langille and I'm inviting Charlie Hunter and we're going to have an all day picnic on Og Pass and Jim is going to fly us in. Will you come?"

"I'll come if you let me pay part of the helicopter."

"I'm having the party, not you. This is my party."

"Who's paying for the helicopter?"

"None of your business. It's my party. Will you come?"

"Well, I don't know. It's kind of hard for me to just buzz off like that."

"I don't know why it is."

"Well, just drop everything and . . ."

"Yeah, that's right, drop everything. Langille's coming, Charlie's coming and Jim's going to fly us in."

"Doggone it. I'll bring some food."

"You'll bring nothing."

"Well, I'll bring a dozen beer."

"You'll bring nothing. You'll come. Will you come?"

"How much is the chopper going to cost?"

"None of your business. Do you always ask all these personal questions of people who ask you out for dinner?"

"No, not always, but sometimes I do."

"Will you come?"

. . . So we went, the chopper came and we all piled in and she explained that old Charlie had hidden one of these glacier boulders (glacier eggs) which are very round.

"Charlie has one up in the woods from Og Pass and if Jim will allow us to bring it out you can help Charlie get it down the mountain."

So we flew in and found a place for the picnic and Jim went away off with his chopper and Lizzie wanted to walk down and look over into Assiniboine Pass and I wanted to go up there to see a whole herd of elk and Charlie went off. (Eileen Langille went with Lizzie; they each had a pack.) We hung some food in a tree and I made a place for a fire and I went up there and by chance Mary Ann, my daughter, and a girlfriend were over at Strom's Lodge by Mount Assiniboine and they came up another pass and I was whistling and screaming at them. (They knew we were going to be there and they were going to come and Lizzie thought that would be alright.)

When I came down she said, "You know, Charlie needs your help."

"What the hell for?"

"To get this rock down the mountain."

So I looked up and there was cursing and swearing up in the bush. There were some big trees and there was an open area, and there was Charlie with this big rock that weighed one hundred and eighty-six pounds, wrapped up in canvas with a big rope on it and he was pulling it through the bush. So I rushed up and said, "Charlie I'll help you."

"I don't need any help."

"Well, alright. When you get the stone down I'll help."

We had to roll it down the mountain and it started rolling and the rope got twisted around my hand and I had to either roll too or get rid of it . . . I don't know how I got rid of it. Then you should have heard the oaths. The cursing and swearing and I was helping him swear.

Then we had to pull it and it weighed a ton. We got it over there and had our nice picnic and laid around the fire and the girls came and I took some pictures.

Jim came with the chopper. He said, "I don't know what we're going to do with Charlie."

"Why?"

"He wants to lift the rock in. The chopper will take his head off. He doesn't realize anything about helicopters you know."

"Did you say anything to Lizzie?"

"Sure, I told her I'd only take him if, when I left, she would look after him."

So I said, "Charlie, come and sit by Lizzie."

"I've got to lift the rock in first."

2

So I went over and I said, "Lizzie, he won't come over here and Jim won't open the door to put the bloody rock in until you get him over here and get him interested. Can you give him some tea or some damn thing or other or tell him a story?"

So she got him away, with bushes between them and the chopper and started some line of B S and so on. I ran over and Jim said, "Alright!"

We put the rock inside and closed it up. Pretty soon Charlie came over . . .

"Where's that Goddamn rock?"

Jim said, "Oh well, we put it in Charlie."

"I wanted to put that in there."

"Well you were busy."

Jim was terrified. Charlie was getting old and he couldn't remember that you have to stay down, he was almost deaf, and Jim didn't want to stop the engine. The rotor was still going. So, we finally got the rock in and Lizzie in and got the whole damn thing back to Banff.

Charlie was living in a little cabin in the dump ground just outside of Banff. You had to unlock the gate with a key to get into his cabin.

We got a truck to come and pick up the rock — damn near tipped the truck over — we got the rock in and dumped it at the gate. It was a city yard distance from the gate to the cabin so I grabbed hold of it and started pulling that rope.

Charlie came up and pushed me away and said, "I'll look after this."

He put that rock in that cabin, right beside his bed, up three or four stairs, one hundred and eighty-six pounds.

He said, "You know, doctor, when I wake up in the night I just put my hand on it and there it is."

That was his rock, brought all the way from Og Pass.

In the course of all this I took one or two shots and I took one of Lizzie standing there all alone on Og Pass with her pack and made a print of it and sent it to Janey and she liked it very much.

Of all the passes she had been on . . .

I said, "Why Og Pass?"

"Because it is my pass. I went over it one of my first times to Assiniboine. I thought it was so beautiful."

Dr. J. S. Gardner

3

CHAPTER II

Early Years

IN THE LATE NINETEENTH CENTURY EUROPE WAS IN THE LAST THROES of the Hapsburg dynasty and Europeans were still dominant politically and culturally. Many Europeans still believed it was only natural and inevitable the world should fall under European domination. While aristocratic Europeans were still living in luxury, however, the rumblings of change could be felt when the Social Democrat Party in Austria won its first seats in the Reichsrat.

At this time, England and the Commonwealth were celebrating the diamond jubilee of Queen Victoria's reign and the European colonies were flexing their muscles causing small wars in many directions.

In Canada, the Klondike gold rush was in full swing in the north. People from all over the world were flocking to its creeks and rivers in the hope of finding a fortune.

It was an age of uncertainty and change, not unlike our own, into which Elisabet von Rummel was born on February 19, 1897, in Munich, Germany. Elisabet's father, Baron Gustav von Rummel, was an officer in the German army and an actor in live theatre in Munich. Her well educated mother, Elisabet (Elsa) Hirth, came of a wealthy publishing family in Munich.

In the summer of 1897 when Elisabet was making her first tentative attempts to sit up alone, events were taking place in far off Canada, in an environment that would one day become more significant to this tiny baby than all the power struggles and rich cultural life of the European continent.

J. Norman Collie, A. Michael and Peter Sarbach spent the summer of 1897 climbing in the Canadian Rocky Mountains. As they rowed across Lake Louise, in the heart of the mountains, and struggled up the glacier and spectacular peak of Mount Victoria, they were unaware that

Elisabet and her Grandmother Hirth.

a small baby in Germany would one day stand on that same summit and find it far more meaningful than the wealth and power into which she had been bred. That event was, however, many years away. While these three intrepid mountaineers struggled across the Victoria Glacier, Elisabet was content to crawl, laugh and be fed by her beautiful mother, the Baroness Elsa von Rummel.

Elisabet (Elsa) Hirth was born in the year 1879 to Elise Knorr and Georg Hirth. Georg Hirth, together with Elise's brother Tomas Knorr, was the publisher of the Jugend magazine and the München Neuste Nachrichten newspaper in Munich. His great wealth enabled him to give Elsa everything money could buy. Elsa grew up surrounded by wealth and culture and also surrounded by the people who created that wealth and culture. Artists and aristocrats of all varieties floated in and out of the Hirth family's life as easily as logs floated down streams in far off Canada. Haus Hirth was the place to go socially.

The social standing of the Haus Hirth made an excellent entrance-way for the handsome Baron von Rummel to come striding into Elsa Hirth's life on the cultural carpet of hospitality. Gustav was a welcome addition to the Hirth family, whose love of the stage was most evident in the names of Elsa's brothers — Siegfried, Oswald, Artur and Walther. Names that came off the operatic stage in the same way as later generations would acquire names from the world of movie queens and kings.

5

The family home in Munich, Germany.

Gustav von Rummel also came of an aristocratic family; one which could trace its lineage back to Josef Rummel, a burger in Nürnberg in 1600.

The romance of Gustav and Elsa culminated in marriage in May of 1896 and conferred upon Elsa the title of baroness. By 1901 three

Gustav and Elsa von Rummel on their wedding day.

little baronesses had been born to Gustav and Elsa, but their marriage ended in divorce in October 1901.

Elisabet was the first of the three daughters born to Gustav and Elsa von Rummel. Johanne Luise was born October 15, 1898, and Eugenie was born March 2, 1901. Three little girls born to a woman who was still only a girl herself, having married at the age of seventeen. Each of the three children were baptised into the Catholic church, as had been Elsa; although Elsa was not the least bit religious.

Famous and wealthy people are, however, no more immune from marital strife than poor people and the Hirth and von Rummel families were no exception.

Not long before Elsa and Gustav married, Elsa's father and mother divorced and Georg Hirth remarried a much younger woman than himself. This marriage resulted in four children who were approximately the same ages as Elisabet, Johanne and Eugenie. Their names were Louisl, Wolfgang, Traudl and Otto, and each became good friends to the three von Rummel children; a friendship which lasted all their lives.

The divorce of Gustav and Elsa von Rummel was rumored to be due to Gustav's interest in the ladies, but this is an unsubstantiated rumor. Elsa's feelings, however, were very hurt by the events surrounding her divorce and she subsequently broke all ties with von Rummel and Elisabet, Johanne and Eugenie were never allowed to see their father nor talk about him again. In spite of the fact Elsa's mother spent many hours arguing the advantages of the three children seeing their father, Elsa would not budge from her decision. It was twenty-five years before Elisabet saw her father again, twenty-seven before Johanne did and Eugenie never did see him again.

Since von Rummel, under the stage name of Gustav Waldau, became very famous throughout Germany and Europe, the girls frequently heard of him, thus, as adults when they wished to see him, he was not hard to find.

Elsa was beautiful, wealthy and endowed with a captivating and charming personality; hence it was not long before another man entered her life. Dr. Fritz Weinmann was a wealthy Jewish pianist with, not only a home in Munich, but a family estate on the edge of the historic Stauberger Lake. It was in this lake, situated near the village of Leoni, the insane German king Ludwig had drowned.

Elsa and Fritz Weinmann were married in April 1903. Most of their short married life was spent in the large house on Weinmann's family estate, together with the three little girls. Mrs. Weinmann, Fritz's mother, lived on the same estate in another house and she became very devoted to Elsa and her daughters; an association which continued until her death sometime after 1936. Elisabet visited her stepgrandmother at that time while on a visit to Germany. Mrs. Weinmann was then very feeble. In this idyllic setting, on the edge of Stauberger Lake, Fritz and Elsa were very happy. Many hours were spent in the beautiful flower gardens of the estate and boating on the lake with the little girls.

During a portion of 1903-04, the family took a tour of Seesbaupt and its mountains. Unfortunately, Elsa and Fritz's happiness was shattered in October 1905 when Weinmann suddenly died of peritonitis.

Three children and two heartbreaks in a short space of time may well have been the motivating force which drove Elsa to travel throughout Europe with her three children and their governess. Inheriting the vast estate of Fritz Weinmann helped to make this possible, although Elsa had money from her father as well. For the next two years Elsa travelled extensively.

While January of 1906 was spent in the Bavarian mountains, Elsa went to Hothalp in July, Leutasch in September, Salzburg in October,

The Weinmann Estate on Stauberger Lake. Johanne, Eugenie and Elisabet.

Munich in December, as well as visits to Geneva, Rome and the Weinmann estate on Stauberger Lake. It was a busy year.

The following year Elsa and her three girls, plus their governess, were not only at Stauberger Lake but spent most of the summer and winter in Berwang, a village in Bavaria where Elsa owned a house. Today Berwang is a busy tourist spot but when Elsa and her children lived there they were the only tourists. This property in Berwang was never sold until after 1966.

Soon a dark, curly headed, good looking man named Robert Basilici entered Elsa's life and in November 1907, they were married.

Basilici, born on August 2, 1882, was a poor Italian painter of nudes and a champion swimmer with a beautiful physique. His parents, Adele and Guiseppe Basilici, lived in Rome near the Coliseum. Their house was small but comfortable and Mrs. Basilici allowed her tame birds to fly around the house uncaged. She became very fond of Elsa's three children and often gave them lovely chocolates.

Elsa may well have met Basilici through her father, as Georg Hirth had published three of Basilici's paintings on the front cover of his Jugend magazine.

Elsa's love of travel was shared by Basilici. Accompanied by the three children and their governess, they continued Elsa's travelling habits. May of 1908 was spent in London, England, June and July on a boat trip to Venice, part of July in Rome and from September on into the next year was spent at Elsa's house in Berwang, Bavaria. By April of 1909 they were in Munich and back to England again from May to August. During this trip to England the three girls took riding lessons at George Welsh's riding school in Shepherdton.

Welsh was an accomplished trick roper as well as a riding teacher. He too was captivated by Elsa's strong personality and the two developed a friendship which was to last many years.

The summer of 1909 Elisabet, Johanne and Eugenie learned to ride horses for the first time and, under George Welsh's watchful eye, they fell in love with the animals that would forever become an integral part of their lives, albeit in a much different setting. Johanne had long since become concerned with the welfare of the beautiful beasts and although very small, would always note how well the horse pulling their carriage was looked after. It was as though her penchant for horses and their welfare came with her when she was born.

Elsa and her entourage always seemed to be on the move. Robert, three children, a governess and the endless chore of seeing to everything while travelling kept them busy. Their touring continued in September of that year and found the family in Berwang, but by November they were in Rome again. The following year a voyage was taken to Turkey from where they narrowly escaped a cholera epidemic. Elisabet developed diarrhea on the train during their escape, but fortunately, it was not cholera.

Elsa's constant travelling was a source of wonder and talk amongst her many friends in Munich and she was frequently teased. One evening, at a dinner party in Munich, a gentleman teasingly said to her: "I know one place where you have not been." That place was Canada and it was not long before the gentleman had sold this wealthy, but unsuspecting, young woman three quarter sections of land in the foothills of the Canadian Rocky Mountains and changed her life forever.

Elsa, Robert and the three girls set sail for Canada in April of 1911, this time without the usual governess and with Elisabet in charge of the tickets. This first trip necessitated a four day train journey from Halifax, Nova Scotia, across the hundreds of kilometres of Canadian soil before the family arrived in Calgary, Alberta. From Calgary a democrat was hired which took them to the little hamlet of Priddis, south of Calgary. Here Elsa and Robert left the three girls at Mrs. Gillespie's boarding house while they went on to the Gate Ranch which Elsa had purchased.

Elisabet, now fourteen years old, Johanne, twelve years old and Eugenie, ten years old, were thrilled with western Canada and the cowboy flavor emanating out of Priddis. Elisabet's perennial curiosity took her into Mrs. Gillespie's aromatic kitchen where she learned to bake bread and do simple cooking chores. At this point in time, Elisabet's cooking knowledge was non-existent due to the kitchen staff, not to mention butlers and other servants, who ran the European households in which she had lived. Mrs. Gillespie was captivated by this curious young baroness who did not know how to cook. Every young girl she knew had learned that art at a much younger age.

The Gate Ranch had been purchased by Elsa from Louis Taylor and it was he who met Elsa and Robert Basilici in Priddis and took them the twenty miles southwest of Priddis to the ranch. Elsa and Robert spent two weeks on the ranch before returning to Priddis where they collected the three girls to take them to the ranch.

Bumping along the rough roads in the democrat, the girls were wide-eyed with wonder as the Rocky Mountains loomed above the foothills on the western horizon. Here, on this most worthwhile of investments, Elisabet, Johanne, Eugenie, their mother and step-father romped and played for one long Canadian summer. By the time they returned to Germany in the autumn, the three girls, at least, had sold their hearts to Canada's foothills country.

CHAPTER III

Gate Ranch

WHILE MEMORIES OF THE WONDERFUL CANADIAN SUMMER FLOATED through their heads, Elisabet, Johanne and Eugenie tried to apply themselves to their studies in the school they attended in Munich. Walking to school with their satchels slung over their arms they talked rapturously of the fun they had had and the hopes of returning to Canada. Many evenings were spent coaxing Elsa and Robert to return to Canada the following summer.

The family did return to Canada the next summer. When they returned they took with them a maid — Anna. "Anna didn't last more than ten minutes" before one of the hundreds of yearning young bachelors to be found on the Canadian frontier, married her. Anna may have been with the Basilici family a year but that is uncertain.

During the summer of 1912, while frolicking in the luxury of a pleasure ranch, the family attended the first Calgary Stampede. George Welsh, the horseman from Shepherdton, England, now working for Elsa on the Gate Ranch, competed in trick roping and won second prize. This stampede was a highlight of the young girls' lives and one which was never forgotten. Elisabet treasured her stampede button for the rest of her life. The Calgary Stampede had further heightened the girls' love of horses and much time was subsequently spent riding in the countryside near the ranch. Since all five members of the family were adventuresome, they enjoyed the riding excursions immensely.

At the time of these summer visits to Canada, the ranch was merely a pleasure ranch. No one in the family knew anything about ranching. George Welsh was hired to look after the horses and do the necessary ranch chores. There was, however, so little for him to do, he took other horses to break for riding to keep himself occupied. It seemed an odd arrangement but rather a necessary one.

Suddenly and dramatically war broke out between Germany and England the summer of 1914 while the family were in Canada at Gate Ranch. Quite unexpectedly the Basilici family were cast adrift into an unknown world where money was not available and hard physical work was necessary. Because Canada was an ally of England the family could not return to Germany and they could not get their money from

Gate Ranch with Niggar John Ridge in background.

Germany. Elsa and Robert hoped the war would not be long but soon the family hung precipitously over the cliff of poverty. The realization slowly dawned on them that their salvation lay in Gate Ranch, so with trepidation they faced the future and grasped the opportunity to earn a living by turning the pleasure ranch into a working ranch. Everyone quickly learned how to work. Elisabet found herself in the kitchen doing all the housework; Johanne and Eugenie preferred to work outdoors with the animals and in the fields, and Elsa and Robert fitted in as best they could.

Not only did no one in the family know anything about ranching, but they knew nothing about cooking and cleaning. The simple introduction to cooking which Elisabet had acquired from Mrs. Gillespie in Priddis was hardly adequate to help once Anna married and moved away. With some effort and a lot of tenacity, the girls and Elsa learned to cook and clean, but it was years before their home matched the cleanliness of their neighbours. Eventually, Elsa became excellent cooking fresh fish.

At first this change in lifestyle was hard and adapting to it was painful. Elsa's adjustment to the new set of circumstances was remarkable. She had spent all her life living luxuriously; doing what she wanted, going where she wanted and buying what she wanted, with servants for every household task. Lack of money had never stood in her way. . . .this very money which brought she and her girls to Canada and changed their lives so dramatically.

Being the eldest of the three girls, Elisabet was more responsible, even more so than her mother. Initially the bulk of the work fell on her shoulders. Many hours were spent struggling within herself over the set of their fortunes and what it was now meaning to her.

No doubt when the First World War was over Elsa planned to return to Germany, but by the time it was possible to return, the ranch and foothills country had become home and the three girls begged Elsa to remain. They were tired of travelling and they loved the ranch life. Although Elsa had a strong, captivating personality, her wealth and position had never required her to stay in one place. Thus staying in Canada, working the ranch, making economic decisions which were totally foreign to her, was very hard. The fact she adapted is a credit to her ingenuity and shows her great strength. The fact, also, her daughters never once heard her complain about the change in her circumstances, gives a picture of a very remarkable woman.

While all five members of the family were adapting and struggling with inner conflicts they were also enjoying themselves in spite of the problems. The hardness of their life was lightened by their own inner resources, their sense of humor, and the culture they brought with them.

Gate Ranch, in the backwoods of Canada, possessed an international flavor. Not only did the log house hold three hundred German books and a piano, but four languages were spoken almost simultaneously within its walls. Robert Basilici spoke French with Elsa, Italian with his cousin (Who stayed a year or two.); the girls spoke English, German, French and Italian (But could not read or write French and Italian.); Elsa spoke French, German, Italian and English and the hired man spoke only English. All of these languages were spoken criss-crossing each other. It was a strange, multi-lingual household. Three young girls, all of whom were baronesses, a rich aristocratic lady (Elsa lost the title of baroness when she married Weinmann.) and an Italian artist, living in a log house with an Englishman as hired hand — in Canada's western frontier, the newly formed Province of Alberta.

Although multi-culturalism was the the norm and fibre of Canada, the unique·part about this household was the whole gamut could be found under one roof.

In spite of her own excellent education, from whence her fluency in languages came, Elsa seemed to have forgotten about her daughters' education after they arrived in Canada. They had arrived without the usual governess and never again had one, nor did the girls attend school once they remained in Canada. Johanne did attend for one day, but when a boy threw rocks at her Elsa said she did not have to go back. Possibly the thought they would be returning to Germany made Elsa less concerned with this lack than she might otherwise have been. By the time she saw the writing on the wall, it was too late. Elsa's own avid interest in everything was, however, transmitted to her three daughters and they always pursued their own avenues of interest throughout their lives.

Elisabet had been a keen student of piano in Germany and did very well. The inability to continue her piano studies always remained a sore point with her. When a piano was later purchased, the opportunities of Europe were not available on the Canadian frontier. While Elisabet's piano studies had to fall by the wayside, her interest in books was still keen and never waned throughout her life. The rich library in the log house in the foothills was a constant source of material to her and her sisters. Her seemingly innate interest in flowers launched her into gardening for which she had a very green thumb. Her friends were constantly getting starter plants from her and these plants always did well.

Johanne and Eugenie were the avid artists, although Elisabet drew as well. The girls spent many hours drawing from their environment. Eugenie had an impressive gift for drawing horses and could easily draw a herd of horses bunched together with all the legs in the picture and in the right place. Eugenie was also very interested in geography and spent hours pouring over maps.

While Johanne never did know the location of the Atlantic or Pacific oceans, she was excellent in mathematics and could easily do calculations in her head. Johanne also had an uncanny ability with horses. They were her consuming interest. Even as a small child she had become very aware of horses and had tender feelings for their welfare. She became involved in breeding and showing equestrian and draft horses, and in judging.

Fortunately, while this multi-lingual family struggled with adaptation to a new life, they were relieved of local anti-German feelings during the war. This was largely due to the fact their mother and stepfather's name was Basilici, an Italian name, and the three girls were known as "the Basilici girls." Later people did know they were von Rummels and baronesses, but they used the Basilici name until adulthood. This was partially due to Johanne and Eugenie being included on their mother's passport. Elisabet had her own passport and when she did leave the ranch, years later, she assumed her proper name of von Rummel, eventually dropping the "von".

Throughout their lives, the girls acquired a variety of names and nicknames. Elisabet was nicknamed Liesel, Lisi and Ish; Johanne was nicknamed Hanni and Bims; and Eugenie nicknamed Geni. Even Elsa who was usually called Mutti, for mother, later was called Omi, the German name for grandmother, when she acquired grandchildren. Eventually, the three girls Anglicized their proper names to Elizabeth, Jane and Nina. Much later the Lisi became Lizzie but that name largely belongs to another part of her life.

CHAPTER IV

Working the Ranch

AS THE FIRST WORLD WAR PROGRESSED THE FAMILY'S ADJUSTMENTS to their new lifestyle on the ranch became even more stressful as Elsa's husband, Robert Basilici, was becoming mentally unstable with unpredictable and occasional violent behavior. These problems culminated when it appeared Elsa and the girls were about to lose the ranch. Elsa had innocently put the ranch into Robert Basilici's name and now he was threatening to take it away from her. Elsa secured a capable lawyer in Calgary who was able to get the deed put into her name due to the fact she had purchased the ranch with her money and paid every bill from her own resources. Fortunately, she had kept all of the bills, thus saving them from further heartbreak.

Towards the end of this period Robert joined the Lord Strathcona's Horse (Royal Canadians) regiment on October 28, 1918, and served with the regiment in Canada until April 7, 1919. His emotional condition continued to be unpredictable in the way he was relating to people.

Also in 1919, Elsa's mother in Germany became very ill so a trip to Germany· was planned. Due to the loss of their money, Elsa sold a lease on the oil rights of the ranch to pay for the trip and thereby secured the money not only for the trip to Germany, but also to purchase a car for the ranch.

The winter in Germany was spent renewing family ties and old friendships. Although Elsa and Robert were still married Robert's emotional instability alienated them from each other so they lived in separate houses in Munich. Elizabeth, Jane and Nina had, by this time, come to love the foothills ranch so deeply they desperately wanted to return to it. Their persistence at returning to Canada forced Elsa to abandon any hopes she may have had of staying in Europe. The family

Liesel on the ranch.

returned to Canada in July of 1920 — in time to nurture more young calves into adulthood.

Robert Basilici did not return to Canada until November 8, 1921. Since he was still emotionally ill he and Elsa secured a legal separation on November 11, 1921, and then on January 23, 1922, Robert sailed from Halifax to Europe. The unfortunate man died October 16, 1929, in Berlin, with cancer of the throat.

The conflicts arising from Basilici's emotional instability hurt Elizabeth tremendously. She carried this pain for many years and seldom spoke of her stepfather. In later years her friends never knew he had been such a large part of her life on the ranch. She would always say it was her mother and the three sisters who came to Canada and worked the ranch. This tactic of not speaking of Basilici was learned from her mother who never spoke of von Rummel after her divorce from him.

Life progressed with and without Robert Basilici. The three girls loved horses so much they eventually decided to raise Clydesdale horses — breaking them for work horses. They invested in a Clyde stallion named "Northern Star" and a bunch of mares and worked at breeding and horse breaking. The three resourceful girls did everything, including breaking the horses to drive and doing their own farrier work. For the farrier work, the girls rigged a trap to front foot the horses for trimming. One girl chased the horse along the side of the corral to where a loop was rigged up on a hook on the corral rail. When the horse stepped in it the other two girls jerked the loop tight. The Clyde would struggle until it fell down. Once down Jane held the horse's head while Liesel tied the three feet together. This horse program was working well and they were almost ready to sell their first team when the advent of the tractor suddenly dropped the bottom out of the work horse market. Teams of horses which would have sold for three hundred dollars had to be sold for forty dollars. This was a heartbreaking loss and a financial tragedy.

After this setback the girls launched out on a program of raising milk cows. Their small herd consisted of ten cows, but each newborn calf was watched with tender loving care. It was not uncommon on cold spring mornings to find four or six calves in the ranch house kitchen all being fed milk laced with a little rum. During calving season in the spring the girls would often find in the fields newborn calves almost frozen. They would then carry them into the house, rub them until the circulation returned and feed them the milk and rum recipe. This careful attention to their small herd saved them from further financial setbacks and provided them with a source of income through the sale of the cream. At that time cream sold for one dollar a gallon.

Although the ranch never turned into a big ranching operation while the girls were managing it alone, it constituted a lot of work for three young baronesses. Jane became the haying expert and loved the activity with a passion. Raking hay was a constant source of joy to her for the rest of her life. Liesel did the cooking and cleaning in the house while Nina became an expert farrier. For many years Jane could not even boil a potato as Liesel had done all the cooking. Elsa, who was totally inept in the kitchen due to her years with servants, eventually mastered the art of cooking. These years working on the ranch bound the three girls and their mother closely together.

The hard work of the ranch was relieved through many avenues of interest. Due to the family's rich, cultural background in the arts, they knew a lot about the theatre and quite naturally created their own entertainment. The three girls, together with their friends, often staged plays for whoever would watch. Frequently their only audience would be their mother and the hired man. Since they lived and breathed horses and all had long hair, Jane and Nina loved to let their hair "get matty like the horses" and in their plays they would play the part of the horses while Liesel played the part of the driver. One play included the girls as cattle rustlers, during which Nina was shot, a tent pitched and a doctor

Nina, Jane, Elsa Basilici and Elizabeth in front of the ranch home.

arrived on the scene who drove off with Nina. Often the audience would be seated in a wagon — reminiscent of box stalls in European theatres.

As well as creating their own theatre, the three girls spent a lot of their free time swimming in the creek. They had a pet calf who would go swimming with them and sometimes they would take their horses. Elsa gave them a tremendous amount of freedom, therefore, their imaginations could run free and run free they did.

The three girls' friendships with the neighbours drew Isabel and Molly Fulton and Constance (Tuck) Phillips into their plays and other fun. All six girls were the same age, liked the same things and

19

remained friends throughout their entire lives. Over the years other friends were acquired as well. Among them were several Stoney Indian people. Gate Ranch was on the Stoney Trail from Morley to the south fork of Sheep Creek, hence many Stonies would stop at the Basilici home and the girls would wind up the gramophone and play records to entertain them. The Stonies particularly liked listening to Caruso sing "Pagliacci" and the part where he laughed in the song. The girls and Elsa frequently enjoyed an evening of fun with the Stonies and there was always a place on the ranch for them to camp and always food to be eaten.

Liesel remained friends with several Stoney people over many years. One gentleman would occasionally borrow money from her and leave his beautiful headdress as collateral. Much later, in 1968, Liesel attended the funeral of Mrs. David Bearspaw, in Morley, who died at one hundred and six years of age.

In 1912 when Johnny Bearspaw met Liesel and her mother he told Elsa, "You pretty near mother-in-law." Johnny Bearspaw was one of the few romantic interests in Liesel's life since many eligible young men had been killed in the war. There was one other fellow in her life during this time who was interested in her for a short time, but somehow nothing came of that interest. Rita Helmer, a ranch wife, who came to know the three girls through the rodeo circuit saw a young man with the girls and their friends at one of the Cochrane rodeos who was decidedly interested in Liesel, but that too disappeared. Later on in her life Liesel did admit to there being a romantic someone, but he was married. Romance eluded the lovely baroness.

During the early years on the ranch it would be hard to find someone with whom Liesel could converse on her own cultural level. While she had left formal education during her teen years, the education she did receive was of a very high calibre and she did speak four languages, played the piano beautifully and could read books of a very high literary standard.

Liesel's farm interests were continually expanding and came to include a Brown Leghorn chicken business. She became very knowledgeable, knowing what to look for in order to have show chickens and entering the chickens in several agricultural shows in Millarville and Calgary. She won many prizes. Also, Liesel and her sisters were actively involved in the Priddis and Millarville annual agricultural show for many years. They entered horses and agricultural products as early as 1918. In time, Liesel became a director of the agricultural show.

Liesel also became a member of the Square Butte School District board. Although her formal education had been cut short, she had read voraciously and enlarged her knowledge in many areas. In spite of these educational pursuits, however, she was always embarrassed to admit she had never finished school. She would not admit this fact to anyone, even when she was over eighty years old.

During the time the three girls were involved in their ranch life, the Canadian government was spending money, time and effort to entice people to emigrate to Canada from Europe. One day an advertisement appeared in a German newspaper accompanied by a picture of the three girls. The advertisement was a promotional gimic depicting German girls ranching in Canada. It was with great surprise the three girls opened a letter from a German relative to find the newsclipping. They had not known about the picture.

Elizabeth, Jane and Nina were being shaped by the Canadian environment and were maturing through the hard, but rewarding ranch life. The problems of adaptation ceased and they settled into the way of life as if they were born to it. Each of the three girls had one distinctive genetic advantage for ranch life — they were all exceptionally physically strong. This physical trait was a great asset to Liesel, not only during ranch days, but later in her life as well.

Each summer from about 1920 to 1932 the girls, together with their friends, took a holiday from ranch life by riding west through the mountains to the Kananaskis Lakes. Several packhorses were laden down with tents and foodstuffs and everyone would swing into the saddle and ride up Sheep Creek Trail to the Burns coal mine. Here they would camp the first night of their journey and from there ride to Elbow Lake, over Elbow Pass and down Pocaterra Creek to a campsite on the Lower Kananaskis Lake close to the ranger's cabin. For ten days they would fish and explore or just enjoy each other's company. Once Elsa accompanied the party and took fresh cream with her. The cream turned into butter by the time they arrived at the Kananaskis Lake due to the jogging of the horse she rode.

The group's return journey was made over Highwood Pass, up Mist Creek and over Rickard's Pass to the Burns mine again and home to take up the reins of ranch work.

While the girls struggled to make the ranch pay, their mother tried to get more of her German money into Canada. During the war she made several trips to New York and developed a strategy to get some money through a gentleman whom she knew in New York. The man would give Elsa some of his money and she would give him some of her money which was still in Germany, but which he was able to get and she was not. Some years later Mr. Harcourt-O'Reilly, a Calgary lawyer, went to Germany and secured more funds for her. Subsequently Elsa and the three girls remained friends with the Harcourt-O'Reilly family for many years.

Life went on, concern with finances, raising horses, cattle and chickens, haying and friendship with neighbours and Stoney Indians, until it achieved a certain secure monotony. Then in 1927 Nina, the youngest, fell in love with Paddy Rodgers and on February 17, 1928, they were married.

Paddy came from a well to do family in the area, was a very likeable chap and brought to the ranch his own cattle. He was also a very brave man to move into the ranch home with four women. The ranch, however, was very much in need of a man to help in its expansion, and the house was large enough to accommodate one more. Everyone got along very nicely.

CHAPTER V

Europe Revisited

IN SPITE OF THE WARMTH AND SECURITY OF HER RANCH HOME, Elizabeth had a great desire to see her father again. Although she was only four years old when her parents divorced, she could still remember something of him. She had also learned about his theatrical activities through newspapers and relatives while still living in Europe. By 1930 her desire to see her father and her homesickness for Europe took her on a trip to Germany in June of that year and on her way Elizabeth visited her mother in New York where Elsa was living and working.

Lisi found her father, Gustav von Rummel, and came to love him. She visited with him on the French Riviera and they also spent several weeks together in Switzerland during July and August. Sometime after Elsa and Gustav's divorce, Gustav had married a beautiful actress named Hertha von Hagen (Who was called My for short. Pronounced "Me.") Lisi also became very fond of My, her stepmother.

While in Europe, Lisi wrote to her family and friends in Canada through postcards.

July 13, 1930. Die Bernina-Bahn, Switzerland.
Am having a simply wonderful time, will write more from St. Moritz. This is more like home, am so happy. Woke up and thought I was at Kananaskis! The air and mountains and such a wonderful trip from Geneva, was really lovely. Only always that cheap feeling about you people. Hope you are all alright.

Love,
Lisi.

July 22, 1930. Restaurant Fuorcla Surlej
2,760 m., Switzerland.
Went up there with Papa, quite a trip, 6 hours. It was lovely,
8,280 feet. Am feeling first rate. Hope you are all well.

All love,

Lisi.

July 30, 1930. St. Moritz, Switzerland.
Am having a wonderful time. We are here for a few weeks,
have also been to the Riveria with my father before that. Am
really a lucky girl so far. Hope you had a good summer. Am
so thrilled about the Election in Canada.

Heaps of love to all,

Lisi.

September found Lisi in Berlin-Charlottenburgg but why she was
there we do not know. Lisi came back from Europe October 11, 1930, to
resume her life on the ranch, but somewhere she picked up a gnawing
desire for a change.

On January 17, 1933, life took on another change for Lisi when
her sister Jane married Joseph Fisher, Jr. Joe's father, Joseph Fisher, Sr.,
was one of the first settlers in the Millarville district a fine
heritage for a colorful foothills cowboy who daringly rode almost-wild
horses to the hitching rail of the Basilici home when courting Jane. It
was a sure way to win the heart of a pretty girl who loved horses. Joe
built a beautiful log house for he and Jane not far from the Basilici
home. When they moved into their house the Basilici home felt bereft
of a valuable member.

By the time Jane married, Nina and Paddy Rodgers had a son,
Michael Gustav, and Lisi had now only a small, cold room in the
upstairs of the ranch house to call her own. While the women always
got along well in the household, Lisi was not needed as she had been in
the past. Not only were there now two men to do the work, but Jane and
Nina were developing lives of their own apart from Lisi. Elsa too, was
busy with her own life. While Elizabeth, Jane and Nina had forced their
mother to return to Canada as a permanent home, they could not stop
her proverbial itchy foot from itching.

Elsa started travelling again with a trip to Victoria, British Columbia, in January 1923. This time she had to travel alone as her three
daughters were immersed in their own lives and were unwilling to
accompany her. The following year Elsa made a journey to Los
Angeles, in the United States, where she stayed for almost three
months. In 1925 she started making frequent trips to New York, which

lasted until 1934, visiting friends and working as tutor and companion to Mike McFadden's teenage children and possibly others. McFadden was a famous dietition, in the thirties, with kitchens for poor people all over New York, which became famous for their wheat porridge.

Elsa was gone so often, once for over a year, that one time when she did come home, Jane wrote a poem in honor of the event. When Elsa did give up her travelling ways, Joe Fisher added a room onto his ranch house for her. Unfortunately, Joe and Elsa never got along and arguments frequently disrupted the household.

By 1936 Nina had been married for eight years and Jane was expecting her second child; Lisi, anxious to see her father again, made another trip to Europe in the spring. Lisi was in Europe from March until, at least mid-summer, but possibly longer.

Prior to leaving for Europe, Lisi had made arrangements with her mother to try and sell the books and furniture which they had left stored in the Wetch storage house in Munich since taking up permanent residence in Canada. While most of Lisi's time was spent visiting relatives, she did go skiing as well and thoroughly enjoyed herself.

Garmisch-Partenkirchen.
Sprung von der Olympiaschauze.
April 4, 1936.
Dear, dear people: Your letters were just lovely again. Many, many thanks. I simply gobble them up and know them nearly by heart. You are right Geni, I get them in a bunch always on Wednesday so don't bother to mail twice a week, just write and mail them whenever you go down. All the news is so nice to hear, am glad the cattle are not too thin. Hope the weather keeps warm. Dear ones, sometimes I get pretty homesick. But I am enjoying it here too. Here at Papa's it is so quiet and peaceful, they are always so kind to me. And we talk of you and the Ranch nearly every night. . . . . I went to see Grosmama Weinmann with Kurt. (ed. Fritz Weinmann's mother and brother.) She is not very well, but her mind is as bright and clear as ever. She was touching, quite blind and has pains but so proud does not complain. Perhaps Mutti you could write her. Kurt is afraid she will not live much longer, is 87 now. She gave me the little painting of Papale as a child. . . . . Have not started at Wetch yet, will do so after Easter but everyone tells me you get nothing for books and furniture these days. . . . .
Heaps of love to you all,
Ish.

Besuchen Sie den Sommer-u. Tirol.
May 6, 1936.
Am staying with Victor for two days. It is just as lovely here
as it was twenty-five years ago. All the family is putting in
spuds today, am going with them. They are awfully nice to
me and remember us all so well.

Love from
Ish.

On June 13th Lisi travelled through Valepp, Spitzensee,
Spitzenkarnm, Schliersee and Rottach to stay with her Uncle Walther
in the Bavarian alps at Grainau.

Walter Hirth, Elsa's brother, lived in a large house which he had
built for his mother, near the village of Grainau. Walther had lost his
fortune in the big inflation during the First World War. He and his wife,
Johanna, had lost their house in Munich, so moved to Grainau where
they operated their home as an exclusive pension for rich friends and
their friends. Haus Hirth of Grainau soon became a cultural retreat such
as Elise Hirth's home had been in Munich. Such notables as Philip
Mountbatten (now Duke of Edinburgh) and Katharine Cornell (the
American actress) came to stay with Walter and Johanna.

The number of guests in Haus Hirth was limited to twenty and
many of these guests performed for each other in the quiet evenings.
Lisi enjoyed the conversations about cultural events and her visit with
her aunt and uncle.

In July Lisi went to Mittenwald and stayed with her father and his
wife, My.

Stayed here for one night with Papa and Mama My, a lovely
spot. Thought of you all day yesterday (race day), hope you
had a good time. How are my nephews? And Bims at home
again I hope and everyone well and happy. I bathed in this
lake, was quite warm.

Heaps of love from,
Ish.

When Jane's son, Peter Hirth Fisher, was born on June 20th in
Canada, Lisi and the relatives in Munich held a large celebration party.

Lisi had returned to Canada by the 15th of August but the winds of
change were blowing strongly and her life was soon to take another
dramatic turn.

CHAPTER VI

The Rocky Mountains

AFTER ELIZABETH'S RETURN FROM EUROPE SHE SETTLED INTO LIFE on the ranch for another year. Although she was needed, it was not the same as when all three of the girls were single. Now there were two men to do the heavy work and both Jane and Nina were busy with families and their lives were revolving more and more around them; with Elsa in New York most of the time, it was only natural Elizabeth should think about doing something independent with her life.

It would be impossible to write of the first forty-one years of Elizabeth's life without mentioning Jane and Nina. Practically all of her early life was interwoven with the lives of her two sisters. During the next thirty years, however, the three sisters led different lives. While Jane and Nina always lived close to each other and their lives intermingled, Elizabeth branched out into a new and different world of which her sisters knew little.

Elizabeth's dream was to work or run a guest ranch in the mountains. In order to fulfill her dream she left her sisters and the ranch and went to the Town of Banff in the Rocky Mountains to see if she could fulfill her dream.

> I just wanted to do something on my own. Perhaps run a guest ranch. I knew how to cook and I knew how to operate a place where there are no stores.

In Banff Elizabeth met Nancy Lyall, the Alpine Club of Canada's Clubhouse hostess. Nancy advised Elizabeth to go and see Jim McLeod of Rocky Mountain Tours (Brewster Transport's opposition) as his wife ran a boarding house where she could stay. Elizabeth did so and moved into McLeod's boarding house in February, soon becoming

Elizabeth on the Bow River. 1938.

part of the family. Jean McLeod, Jim's daughter, and Elizabeth became very good friends in spite of the sixteen year age difference. As well, Elizabeth met Muriel Gratz, a Banff school teacher, and Aileen Harmon, who worked for Banff National Park. All three girls became close friends to Elizabeth, a friendship which lasted for the rest of her life.

While in Banff Elizabeth, always an enthusiastic reader, spent time in the Alpine Club library.

> I remember that lovely room, the library in the Club-
> house. . . . Nancy took me up there and it was just wonder-
> ful. They had many, many books then.

As well as visiting the Clubhouse library, Elizabeth gradually became known to the local populace. Banff was a small place in 1938, so it was not hard for a newcomer to become known. Ike Mills, one of the many colorful characters in Banff, became a friend.

One day when Elizabeth was out walking she took a short cut through Mills' corral. Just as she was closing the gate Ike drove up and grunted: "Miss Rummel, caught you trapping again." It was typical of Mills to tease people he liked and it was not hard to like Elizabeth.

Once when Elizabeth was visiting Margarite Rutherford in her store, Margarite told her about Mount Assiniboine, showing her pictures of the Matterhorn-like mountain and Erling Strom's cabins. Elizabeth quickly became very intrigued and asked about the possibility of working for Strom. In the spring she found Erling Strom who was staying at the Dallas House, owned by Sam Evans, on the Cave and Basin Road. Strom was sitting in his room writing a letter when he heard a knock on the door.

> Come in, said I as I turned around. In came a very good looking lady about my own age. She introduced herself as Elizabeth von Rummel. Her slightly German accent gave her away and my Norwegian one probably did the same thing. We spent an exceedingly pleasant half hour together, getting acquainted and it was agreed that she should leave for Assiniboine with Chuck, Chow and myself two or three days later. Typical of both Elizabeth and myself, we forgot to discuss a salary.

In the summer of 1938 an excited Elizabeth rode into Mount Assiniboine to work as chambermaid, hostess and guide. In all of her wildest dreams, Elizabeth could never have visualized how much her life was going to change.

*   *   *

Getting Chow on a horse was not a simple matter, but once in the saddle he sat there for the next seven hours with only one stop in the middle. He had never ridden before and was over sixty years old. Leave it to the Chinese. I don't think there is a race in the world able to take physical punishment better than they. Along the way I would turn in my saddle once in awhile and ask how he was getting along. The answer was always the same.

"Just fine Mr. Strom, just fine."

We rode all the way to Brewster Creek cabin, a good twenty miles. By that time we had to lift Chow off the saddle. He could not stand on his feet, but was hanging onto Chuck and myself saying, "Just a minute please."

We carried him over to the corral fence where he could hang onto the top rail while we unpacked the horses. That done, we brought Chow into the cabin. He could stand by this time and when he discovered the kitchen stove he could not get to it and build a fire fast enough. Chuck brought him some wood and I got a pail of water from the creek. Lizzie, who was in as good shape as any of us, made up the beds from a stack of blankets left on the mouse-proof kitchen table in the fall. We all slept well that night.

Chow was pathetically stiff the next morning, but climbed up in the saddle while we were packing four or five horses. We had a good trip that day and even Chow enjoyed it.

Erling Strom

*   *   *

Mount Assiniboine, rising 3,618 metres from sea level, was often called "The Matterhorn of the Canadian Rockies" due to its similarity to the Swiss mountain. While the name Assiniboine came from the Assiniboine Indian tribe and means "stone-boiler", the Indians' name for the mountain was "the Cloudmaker." Elizabeth soon learned the aptness of the name.

By the time Elizabeth rode into the Assiniboine area, it had been visited by many people and Erling Strom had been there for ten years operating the Mount Assiniboine Lodge. The usual route into the mountain, in 1938, was from Banff, along Brewster Creek, over Allenby Pass (formerly Brewster Pass), down the pass to Bryant Creek and up over Assiniboine Pass. While the mountain is thirty-seven aerial kilometres southwest of Banff, it is fifty-six kilometres by trail via this route.

The Canadian Pacific Railway had previusly built a Halfway Cabin along Brewster Creek and it was here Strom, Chuck, Chow and Elizabeth stayed the first night of their journey. While the first day's ride was gradually uphill, although long, the second day's ride was more arduous as thirty-five switchbacks on the Allenby Pass Trail had to be negotiated before plunging down into Bryant Creek and then the hot climb commenced up the deceptive Assiniboine Pass.

Seen from below, along Bryant Creek, this pass appears to be relatively low, but somehow when climbing up it is a hard and usually hot, sweaty trip for horse or hiker. It is always worth the effort, however, and as Elizabeth came over the crest of the pass and around the corner, Mount Assiniboine suddenly loomed in all its snowclad majesty before her. Like the many people before and the ones who came after to see this mountain, it worked its majestic and mysterious wonders on Elizabeth and was forever after in her heart.

Sitting at the bottom of this imposing mountain was crystal clear Lake Magog and along its shore were the cabins and lodge which Strom leased from the Canadian Pacific Railway. Riding towards this beautiful lake with Mount Assiniboine rising behind it, Elizabeth had no idea of the rich background of the area, but she did know it was one of the most beautiful sights she had ever seen.

"Everything just clicked," and before long Elizabeth knew the area well; its five sparkling lakes, the flower strewn meadows and the scenic alpland completely caught her heart. The mountain itself, rising 450 metres above the surrounding peaks drew her eye irresistibly and

30

cast its charm upon her. It was in this spectacular setting that Elizabeth found her forté and her natural ability of discernment and wisdom touched the people around her.

*   *   *

Lizzie proved to be a perfect hostess at Assiniboine. Her wonderful German background, combined with what life on a ranch in Alberta had added, made it possible for her to cope with anything from entertaining guests to saddling horses, making beds or helping Chow in the kitchen. Nobody surmised that she could use the title of baroness. . . . . She kept that dark in Western Canada, which was probably just as well.

Erling Strom

*   *   *

Ray Heimbecker, a shy, quiet, seventeen year old lad from Okotoks, a small town south of Calgary, also spent the summer of 1938 at Mount Assiniboine Lodge. Heimbecker was the joe-boy, but often his heart was not in it.

*   *   *

One day he was sitting in the kitchen peeling potatoes from a great bucket (Any other lad would have been out fishing.), the corners of his mouth were right down on the ground. Elizabeth looked at him.

"Ray, what's the matter?"

"I may as well get out of here anyway. I am not earning anything and I don't think I'm doing much good, and who in hell wants to peel potatoes for the rest of their lives?"

Elizabeth looked at him, eyes brimming with affection, and said, "Well, I don't know. You sure peel them nicely. You have a nice pair of hands. That is more than some people got."

"What do you mean?"

"Look, the way you peel those potatoes, you could be a wonderful surgeon."

"Yeah, I haven't even finished grade twelve properly."

"Well, you could go back and go to school. What's the matter with you? Come on."

"Oh. . . ."

Dr. J. S. Gardner

*   *   *

Ray Heinbecker did go back to school and finish his grade twelve and went on to university where he received several medical degrees and became one of Canada's top, foremost surgeons, doing original research work on blood clotting.

Elizabeth's empathy and encouragement touched Ray Heimbecker and her entertaining abilities touched the guests.

While most of the guests rode horses to the various lakes in the Assiniboine area, Elizabeth always walked. The guests would set off for the day with a packhorse as well as their saddle horses and in the packbox would be a frying pan, tea billie and lunch for everyone. Arriving at the lake of their choice, Elizabeth would build a small fire and fry the fish which the guests caught, brewing tea to go with the lunch from the packbox. Leaving the guests to continue fishing, Elizabeth would walk back to the lodge, set the dinner table and help the cook prepare dinner. It was a very busy but exhilarating summer.

If occasionally guests wished to go hiking, Elizabeth would take them on the alpland walk up Nub Mountain, or to the many beautiful lakes. She was always interested in the flowers and under the tutelage of a guest, a banker from Victoria, British Columbia, who was also the president of a rock garden society, she started a collection of pressed flowers, learning their Latin names and the various identifying techniques.

*　　　*　　　*

When the day of departure came in the fall, we figured out how much was left in the bag when all the bills were paid, and the rest of the help taken care of. It was not much. I suggested dividing it in three. One third for the camp, one for Elizabeth and the last third for myself. Lizzie thought that very generous and was more than satisfied and so was I. We had all had a wonderful summer and that was the most important.

Erling Strom

Elizabeth on top of Wedgewood Mountain looking north.

After this summer at Mount Assiniboine, Elizabeth returned to the ranch and her little room upstairs in the old ranch house where Nina and Paddy were raising their son Michael. Strom, however, had invited her back to Assiniboine for the next year's spring skiing.

The spring of 1939 was the first time Elizabeth had been on skis in many years and she said, "I couldn't ski for sour apples." Because she had "heard about these horrible trips with Strom" she was hesitant to go with him. In spite of her hesitancy, she did go and managed the two day ski trip into Mount Assiniboine, met Jackrabbit Johannson, who was there as an honored guest of Strom, and learned a little more about skiing.

Jackrabbit and Strom were, at this time, teaching the telemark turn which was just being introduced into Canada, but Elizabeth had so much trouble learning the Christiane that she never learned the telemark turn. Elizabeth used touring skis, a wide ski with edges, and linefelt harness.

Every year Strom held a big ski race with prizes and trophies for each event. One of the events was a race around Lake Magog. Strom set up a table in front of the lodge, listed the participants names on a sheet of paper and sent the skiers off at timed intervals. Strom also raced. He would always be the last one to take off but the first one back!

Everyone skied that race, including the cook. In 1939 Ruth Vernon-Wood beat all the females in the race and took home all the trophies. While Elizabeth skied in the race she was still a beginner and far from ready to take home any trophies. It was, however, a thrill to particpate and be part of the comraderie.

In later years Elizabeth was grateful for the opportunity to ski in Strom's race as it was the last time Strom ran the lodge for spring skiing. Lift tows were making their debut into the skiing world and touring was fast declining as a profitable venture. Elizabeth's name can still be found carved into a log in the lodge.

In the summer Elizabeth returned to Mount Assiniboine to work for Strom and continued to do so until the end of the summer of 1941. By that time she could see the necessity of branching out if she wished to realize her dream and have a place of her own.

CHAPTER VII

Climbing, Skiing and Lake Louise

NOT LONG AFTER LIZZIE WENT TO THE MOUNTAINS TO WORK, SHE became involved in ski touring and mountain climbing. During the winter of 1939-40, when she was living at McLeod's boarding house, she started going up on Mount Norquay to practise skiing. Her natural strength, which was nurtured during her life on the ranch, helped her become a strong skier. Sam Evans said, "She was a good skier. She could keep going."

The spring of 1942 Lizzie attended the Alpine Club's Little Yoho ski camp as hostess. She acquired this position through her friend Sydney Vallance, a Calgary lawyer. Although the participants in this ski camp dwindled to a mere ten persons, and Lizzie was not actually needed, Vallance didn't want to disappoint her, so she was included as a favor to him. Ken Jones was the cook for the camp and went into the Alpine Club's Stanley Mitchell Hut, in the Little Yoho Valley, in Yoho National Park, with Lizzie on March 30th to set up the camp. The camp ran from April 4th to 12th and Lizzie was able to ski with the group frequently.

* * *

Peter Vallance was along that time and my kid brother Norman, and the two Hartley sisters and others. Prosperity Hill is the hill just before Duchesnay Lake and it was hard going. A road had been made in as far as there, that is why the trail is so wide today.

When we came out the snow was so rotten it took sixteen hours to get to the truck near the dividing of the waters. It had rained and rained. The Hartley girls were bugging me about having to catch their train about one o'clock to get to work the next day. Finally we got to Takkakaw Falls about two in the afternoon, and I was sweating like a bull. I had Lizzie's and my own pack as Lizzie was breaking through too. Finally, I had had enough and I threw my ski poles in the air and let go a blast of real, honest to goodness Canadian cuss words.

Lizzie said later, that sure slowed things up. Things were very quiet after that. Those Hartley girls never complained anymore after I exploded.

Ken Jones

*   *   *

During Lizzie's involvement in mountain climbing adventures, she climbed the Devil's Thumb on Mt. White at Lake Louise (2,458 meters) with Al Johnston, Edward Feuz and Janette Farman. When she was working near Lake Louise she participated in climbs with the Alpine Club of Canada during the annual summer camp at Consolation Lakes (July 19 to August 1, 1942). She climbed Eiffel Peak at Moraine Lake (3,084 meters) for her graduation climb as a full member of the Alpine Club. She also climbed Mount Victoria (3,464 meters) with Walter Feuz and Eleanor Asling.

While little is known about Lizzie's climbing exploits, even less is known about her summer at Temple View Bungalow Camp which was situated two kilometers east of the Village of Lake Louise. The camp was owned by Emil Skaren and managed by Mrs. Skaren. Mrs. Skaren, however, left much of the management up to Lizzie.

In a letter to her friend Sydney Hollander of Baltimore, Maryland, Lizzie explained her reasons for being at Lake Louise.

> I felt I simply had to do something for myself. . . . . I will
> learn a lot this summer about running a camp and all will
> help for my plans for the future.

Although Lizzie felt it was unlike her to be "hemmed in by a highway" her goals were becoming clearer.

From this learning situation Lizzie moved into the management of Skoki Lodge in June 1943.

Skoki Lodge is a beautiful log lodge eighteen kilometers from the Village of Lake Louise and is reached by a mountain trail which wanders through flower strewn meadows, climbs over Boulder Pass (2,308 meters) to Ptarmigan Lake, and then over Deception Pass (2,475 meters) with its spectacular view of five alpine lakes. The lodge is at an elevation of 2,400 meters and is situated at the base of Skoki Mountain with a marvelous view of Pika Peak. The Skoki area is a hiking and ski touring paradise.

Skoki Lodge was the dream of Cyril Paris and Cliff White, Sr. These two men skied into the area around 1929 at the suggestion of the Swiss guides from Lake Louise. They saw the potential of the Skoki area for a ski resort and during the fall of 1930 built the first cabin at Skoki. By 1932 Peter and Catharine Whyte had joined them in the business and eventually The Ski Runners of the Canadian Rockies Limited was formed. Cliff White asked Sir Norman Watson to join the company in 1935; by 1945 Sir Norman Watson was the sole owner of the company. This gentleman subsequently changed the name to The Ski Club of the Canadian Rockies Limited (S.C.C.R.).

Sir Norman Watson was a wealthy Englishman who made his money in the airplane factory business in England. Skoki Lodge, Temple Chalet, which was halfway along the trail to Skoki, and the Lake Louise Ski Lodge (now the Post Hotel) in Lake Louise Village, were all eventually owned by Sir Norman Watson. These businesses were like a hobby to Sir Norman, as he was affectionately called.

Sir Norman did want the ski business to become a big development but, unfortunately, he was thirty years ahead of his time. This eccentric, cultured Englishman did not, however, understand the impracticality of some of his ideas. He envisioned a mountain life as in Switzerland, with cattle grazing in the valleys near the lodges, but without regard to wild animals such as grizzly bears and wolverines who may have enjoyed a meal of beef.

Muriel Gratz, Lizzie's school teacher friend from Banff, who knew Sir Norman well could not quite imagine cowboys like Bill Bagley and other diehard trailhands of the day milking cows.

As well, Sir Norman had no idea of how to cope with the day to day running of a mountain lodge in Canada. While he brought lovely carpets and a beautiful full length mirror to Temple Chalet, he did not understand that what was needed was a water system that didn't freeze and a sewer system that drained properly. In the winter the freezing of the water system at the chalet created endless headaches for the management.

Sir Norman also bought a very large carpet for the Lake Louise Ski Lodge which turned out to be too large for the room. The solution, to his way of thinking, was not to cut the carpet, but to remove one wall of the lodge so the carpet would fit as one piece.

Living in a luxurious home in England, with a butler at his service, Sir Norman was not accustomed to closing doors behind himself. On one occasion Muriel Gratz returned home from her school teaching in Banff, to find Sir Norman and Lizzie huddled around the stove in the kitchen — it was thirty-five below zero outside — with the front door wide open. Sir Norman just never closed a door.

In 1946 Jim Deegan, one of Lizzie's packers, was having dinner at Temple Chalet, where Sir Norman usually stayed, and recalled sitting down to dinner with everyone waiting for Sir Norman. Sir Norman arrived downstairs and made a grand entrance into the dining room, dressed in a purple velvet dinner suit, purple velvet tie and a monocule with a purple velvet string attached, and a pair of old, worn out mocassins on his feet!

Prior to Sir Norman Watson's involvement in Skoki Lodge and following the completion of the first cabin, the first guests to the lodge arrived in the spring of 1931 for skiing. Russell Bennett and his family from Minneapolis immediately fell in love with the lodge and the Skoki alplands. On their return to Minneapolis they extolled its virtues to Henry Kingman, who immediately left for the Canadian Rockies and was staying in Skoki Lodge only three weeks after Bennett's departure. These two men remained ardent Skoki fans and subsequently became great friends with Lizzie, returning again and again, summer and winter, to enjoy the spectacular beauty of the area.

By 1933 Jim Boyce, who had arrived in Banff the same year Lizzie first came to Canada, had joined Peter and Catharine Whyte at the lodge as cook, but soon took over the management of the operation. Boyce was a very industrious man and an excellent craftsman in log building. He built many of the log cabins in the Lake Louise area, including the first cabins at Lake O'Hara, the Lake Louise Trading Post (now Deer Lodge) and the Lake Louise Ski Lodge.

Boyce took the roof off the first cabin at Skoki, added a second story and more cabins. By 1936 he had installed a light plant and hot showers in the engine shed with electric lights throughout the lodge. The electricity was produced by a gasoline engine which was started by a twenty-two kilogram battery. These batteries had to be packed in on the backs of hardy men on skis in the winter months and by horse in the summer, together with all the supplies for the camp.

Not only were the packers hardy people but the people who ran the lodge had to be hardy as well. Like a bunch of young grizzly bears, they charged over the mountain passes and through the valleys with sixteen to forty-five kilogram packs on their backs, with all manner of foodstuffs protruding from the top. Crates of eggs and butter, hind quarters of beef and huge turkeys were seen thundering down the trail from Lake Louise to Skoki Lodge. Many times the pack dwarfed the packer. These men, whether packing or building, were made of hardy and tough fibre and all of these people paved the way for an exceptionally strong, middle-aged baroness.

Elizabeth, the baroness, who was never called baroness in Canada, was busy working parttime for Eleanor Asling at the Mountain Inn, a small hotel across from the Lake Louise railway station, and skiing in the area the winter of 1942-43. The Mountain Inn was a busy place as it was not only a hotel, but also the post office, grocery store and restaurant. It was a place which local people frequented and a lot of gossip was passed around. Lizzie was in the right place to hear Jim Boyce was dissatisfied with Skoki Lodge.

Since the Second World War was in progress, it was hard to get guests for the lodge and make ends meet. Lizzie, ever eager for a new adventure, became curious as to what Skoki Lodge was like and if maybe it might be the place for her. Since her skiing was improved from her many trips in the area, she felt ready to tackle the long trip into Skoki Lodge, albeit she was far from being an excellent skier.

With a pack on her back and Joe Tismackie in front with a huge turkey weighing down his rucksack, Lizzie skied into Skoki the winter of 1943.

> And I followed that fellow and I fell and I got up, and I fell and I got up. I couldn't ski for sour apples. And I got to Skoki and you (Jim Boyce) came out the door with this hot rum. You bent down and undid my skis. I'll never forget that. That's real hospitality.

Lizzie stayed one week at Skoki Lodge and was "thrilled about the whole thing." Undaunted by her ability to fall when on skis, Lizzie skied back into Skoki at Easter, by herself — much to Boyce's surprise.

This was the beginning. When Boyce left Skoki that spring, Lizzie tackled Sir Norman Watson and asked if she could lease the lodge.

At that time all of the ski lodges in North America, except Skoki Lodge, were closed due to the war. The fact there were no winter roads to Lake Louise, just train service from Banff, made the area relatively isolated and no one could be found to operate the lodge. Sir Norman preferred to have the lodge open as his dream for a series of lodges was still very much in his mind. Although the financial situation looked glum, Sir Norman took Lizzie on at Temple Chalet in the spring and then leased Skoki Lodge to her in June for one dollar a year.

Thus, this intrepid lady was launched on yet another adventure — at the age of forty-six.

CHAPTER VIII

Lizzie at Skoki Lodge

LIZZIE'S OPERATION OF SKOKI LODGE BECAME A HIGHPOINT NOT only in her life but in hundreds of other people's lives as well. It was here the nickname of "Lizzie" came to be used more frequently. While many of her friends and acquaintances still called her Elizabeth ("Well, she was a baroness" Jim Deegan said.), a greater number affectionately called her Lizzie, and it was this nickname with which she became most wellknown.

Years later she was asked by Jon Whyte how she spelled her name; with a "s" or a "z". She asked what he wanted to know for and when he told her he was compiling photos to be hung in Skoki Lodge, she spluttered, "In the backcountry I was Lizzie! Lizzie. Always. Never anything else."

Lizzie she was and more particularly so from this summer of 1943 onwards.

The first thing Lizzie did when she acquired Skoki Lodge was to secure Ray Legace at Lake Louise to be her outfitter and pack in her supplies by horse during the summer months. Legace remained as her outfitter throughout the whole time she managed the lodge.

This first summer Lizzie also secured Maudie Glaister, the daughter of an old friend in Millarville, to work for her. Each year Lizzie had to scout around and hire a cook, chambermaid and general maintenance man. The maintenance man would chop wood, haul water, shovel roofs and maintain the light plant.

One of Lizzie's best friends was Cliff White, Sr., who would frequently bring up her staples from the railway station at Lake Louise

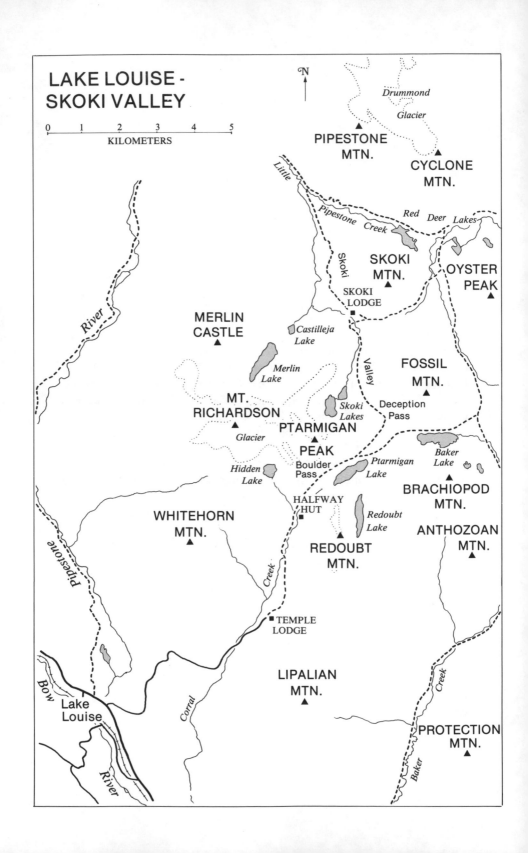

to Temple Chalet. Cliff was the only man who would not tell her "grizzly stories that would make your hair stand on end." He was "just wonderful" and would only caution her "to just be careful."

Underneath the dining room of Skoki Lodge was a cold root cellar in which to store food. Lizzie filled it with bags of potatoes, flour and other supplies, which she did not want to become frozen in the winter or which she wished to keep cool in the summer.

Initially, Lizzie barely broke even financially, but she loved the life. During the war years it was hard to get food because of the rationing but she managed to survive with the same food concessions granted to restaurants and each fall Ken Jones and his friends would go into Skoki to cut wood for the following winter.

During the winter months Lizzie hired young fellows to act as packers for the meat and perishable supplies which had to be brought into the lodge. One year Jack Chisholm was her packer and in 1946 Jim Deegan took on the job. Deegan was a young fellow, about twenty years old, fresh out of the armed forces and recently recovered from war injuries.

*   *   *

I remember I first met Lizzie in 1943 when I was on embarkation leave from the navy, through my uncle Beef Warner, a warden at Lake Louise. She was at Temple. The next time I met her I was out of the navy and looking for a job. I got a ride up to Temple Chalet on the snow cat and skied into Skoki alone with seventy-five pounds of butter for Lizzie, and I got a job as her backpacker.

The whole winter of 1946 I backpacked into Skoki almost every day. The lodge was not busy until Easter time but people did come on weekends. Sometimes I packed from Temple Chalet and sometimes from Lake Louise train station.

Going from Skoki Lodge to Temple Chalet I took one hour to the top of Deception Pass and a half hour from there to Temple. Once a month I had to carry in two fifty pound batteries for the light plant. Going up Deception Pass was hard. I would go a ways and then lean on my ski poles for a rest. Often halfway to the pass, when Lizzie was with me, she would say, "Take that pack off and I'll carry it to the top." She was an amazing woman.

Sometimes she would bawl the heck out of me.

"Gosh, get off the back of my Goddamn skis. We used to kill people in Germany for that."

In those days I was just like a young grizzly.

About every one and a half months I would pack in a quarter of beef. About one hundred and fifteen pounds they would weigh. The leg would stick about three feet above the top of my head. One time I fell when I was halfway down Deception Pass and the leg of beef knocked me out cold with my head between my skis. It was two hours before I came to and dragged myself down to Skoki Lodge.

Every week there was one hundred pounds of potatoes to be packed in, in a big sack strapped onto my Trapper Nelson pack, and seventy pounds of eggs. Lizzie kept the meat in the pantry behind the kitchen where it froze.

The cook that winter was Lillian Lancaster. Lillian had no fear in spite of the fact that she did not know how to ski. On the way from Skoki Lodge to the top of Deception Pass I had to teach her to ski. From there she took forty-five minutes* to reach Lake Louise.

Miss Lancaster made beautiful flapper pie, but it seemed that every time she made it I had to syphon gas from the motor of the gas operated generator and my mouth was so full of the taste of gas that I couldn't eat the flapper pie. I guess it was one of those Murphy laws because flapper pie was my favorite.

Backpacking was just part of the job. I also had to chop wood, shovel roofs and haul six pails of water from the creek every morning before breakfast. The firewood was awful stuff. . . .had to have five or six wedges in it to get it to split. It did not burn well either.

I had lots of adventures in there at Skoki.

One time when I was going from Skoki to Louise, it was late in the season, I got to Ptarmigan Lake and stopped to rest on my ski poles and they just went down, down, down, right into the lake. Boy did we every pussyfoot across that lake! Had a heck of a time getting across.

I remember Herman Gadner who got killed on Little Richardson. He was quite a dare devil. Once he was being photographed by a Toronto Star photographer on the top of Mount Redoubt, on a cornice overlooking Redoubt Lake. There was a sheer two thousand foot drop below the cornice and Gadner just got out on the cornice and did ski turns — being photographed all the time.

Well, that light plant used to cause a lot of headaches. It acquired some pretty powerful names, which could not be used when there were ladies present. It used to heat water for showers which were in the engine shed, but by the time Lizzie was at Skoki it was only used for lights. Every night at six o'clock I had to start it up. It was not too noisy because the engine was muffled.

Yes, I always called her Elizabeth. Lizzie was too informal for someone of that breeding. Most people in those days called her Elizabeth.

Yes, I went back into Skoki after my twentieth birthday bash in Banff* but I didn't just carry that crate of eggs. I had about twenty pounds of mail on top of the eggs as well. I got into Skoki about eight o'clock at night and it was pitch black. I had got to know the route pretty well. It was all flagged out and I knew how many paces it was between each flag. There wasn't much to think about except what the condition of Deception Pass would be.

The winds off Ptarmigan Peak would sing me a beautiful song. . . .just like an orchestra. Then about halfway down the pass I could see the lights from the lodge, just like a beacon, and Elizabeth would be there waiting for me.

She never had to go looking for me but one time she had to go and look for Bill Black's outfit. He was the warden stationed at Cyclone Cabin on the Red Deer River. He and his wife were in there all one winter. This time Bill brought in his mother-in-law who had a club foot. It was her first time on skis and she did not manage them at all, so Elizabeth and I had to rescue her on a toboggan.

I went in there to Skoki Lodge about the first of February and worked until the first of June.

Elizabeth was a darn good friend and we remained friends.

Jim Deegan

*   *   *

Lizzie's first ski guide was Johnny Monod who guided for her the first winter she was at Skoki Lodge and in other years as well. In 1949 he was still guiding for her although at that time she had her own guides' licence. Lizzie, however, was not always able to act as guide due to her many responsibilities.

From 1944 to 1948 Lizzie had a ski guide's licence and in 1946-47 and 1950-51 a National Parks' licence. Her guides' licence was only for a thirty kilometer radius of Skoki Lodge. An area which included Douglas Glacier (Bonnet Glacier on the present topographical maps), Merlin Ridge, Skoki Mountain, Fossil Mountain and Deception Pass. Riel Charette and Ken Jones did guiding for Lizzie as well.

In 1947 Lizzie, accompanied by Georgia Englehart and Tony Cormwell, made the first ascent of Mount Drummond. When the party had crossed the glacier Georgia and Tony said to Lizzie, "You go ahead, we've done so many first ascents." This enabled Lizzie to be the first on the summit of the mountain. Although she admitted it was just a scramble, it was a high point in her life which she remembered forever after and for which she was listed as leading the party in the Climbers' Guide to the Rocky Mountains South.

A number of first ascents were also made under the guidance of Johnny Monod.'

April 18, 1949.
First winter ascent of Cyclone Ridge. Traverse of Drummond Glacier, ascent of Drummond North Peak. Excellent

43

downhill on the glacier, but return exceptionally difficult!
Guest Register Skoki Lodge

A few days after the foregoing ascent, the summit of Mount Lychnis via Douglas Glacier was made in four hours from Skoki Lodge, in beautiful snow conditions. Lizzie was on both of these ski trips.

Again, on April 28th, another first winter ascent was made. This time it was Pika Peak in three and one-half hours from Skoki Lodge to the summit via Merlin Lake. There was good skiing although the "weather wasn't much with occasional snow."

Skiing was the most popular sport at Skoki during the Second World War. Skoki's skiing popularity exceeded that of Mount Assiniboine, due to it being a one day ski trip into Skoki, against the two day trip into Mount Assiniboine.

While most people were using sealskin climbing skins on their skis, Lizzie had made herself some canvas creepers, for economic reasons.

Each year at Skoki a race was held called the Rankin Cup. It was a downhill slalom ski race on the slopes of Pika Peak. A cross-country race from Skoki Lodge to Lake Louise was also held which was called Sir Norman Watson's Race.

Dealing with snow conditions was a constant problem for Lizzie. She learned about snow from the people with whom she came into contact. Erling Strom had taught her and she had a book called "Snow Structure and Ski Fields" which she called her Bible and read religiously. In all the years Lizzie was in the mountains there was never an accident involving her guests. Other people who had been at Skoki, however, had met with accidents. In 1933 Mr. Paley had been killed in an avalanche on Fossil Mountain. Lizzie was often asked, "Aren't you afraid of Paley's ghost?"

"No," she would answer, "when I hear that swish beside me, I think he is protecting me."

At first the ski season and the hiking season were separated by a couple of months, but eventualy Lizzie was at Skoki eight months of the year. She would go home to the ranch or McLeod's boarding house at the end of October, then back to Skoki in February. One year Lizzie and her packers packed in all the season's supplies on their backs in twenty-seven days.

"It is a joy when you are in shape."

During the war a lot of young flyers from Claresholm and other bases would go to Skoki on their forty-eight hour leave. They were mainly British fellows who had learned to ski in Switzerland. The flyers would arrive in Lake Louise by train at four o'clock in the morning, ski into Skoki, stay that night in the lodge, ski out the next day and catch the train back to their base.

Lizzie charged nine dollars a night, with meals, and did not have a reservation system. People just came and there was always room.

As the years rolled by more and more people came from far and near. The Sydney Vallances, the Bennetts, Kingmans, and Arnold Brigden and his wife. Brigden operated the Winnipeg branch of Brigdens Ltd., a photo engraving firm. Both he and his wife were highly individualistic. His interest in plants far exceeded a layman's and did much to help Lizzie identify and learn the proper Latin names for many plants. Brigden took many excellent photographs and often sent copies to Lizzie. He and his wife spent many summers hiking and climbing in Banff National Park and among his friends was the famous Canadian painter Lawren Harris.

Harris was also a guest at Skoki Lodge. Later, when Lizzie was working in the Vancouver area, she visited Harris and his wife in their home. Harris and his wife kept up their friendship with Lizzie over the years and their Christmas cards to her depicted the special place she came to have in their hearts.

Dear Elizabeth —
It was so good to see you and to be with you — you are one of the special people bless you —

Love from
Lawren and Bess.

A number of the guests at Skoki Lodge were Alpine Club of Canada members, many of whom were also friends of Lizzie. Aileen Harmon and Muriel Gratz spent many, many weekends and holidays at Skoki with Lizzie. As well, Lizzie's sisters went with their families, and Elsa Basilici, her mother went a few times too. These occasions were always special treats to Lizzie as she missed the close family contact she had enjoyed for so many years.

Guests went back year after year. Not only was it the area which attracted them, but Lizzie attracted them as well.

*   *   *

I think I have known Lizzie all my life. My father, Sydney Vallance, did her legal work and we were in the mountains. My parents knew her as a friend. When I was in high school I used to go up at Easter to Temple and we would see Lizzie because she was running Skoki Ski Lodge and she would come over to Temple from Skoki to pick up a load of goods. Crates of eggs and things. You would see her going off on her skis carrying ninety pounds. I remember saying what a fantastic woman she was; built just like a horse. I expect that is what crippled her up in later years.

When I got married we went in and spent a few days of our honeymoon at Skoki but she was gone by then. I never stayed there when she was there.

She was wonderful.

Peter Vallance

*   *   *

I don't remember when I first met Lizzie. I would be in my teens. She always called me Jeanie; the only person who ever called me Jeanie.

I worked for her in the winter of 1946. My husband was overseas and I was working for Sir Norman at Temple Chalet and she came in one night and was going to stay overnight and ski into Skoki the next day. I was doing letters for Sir Norman. While she was there that night she got a wire from her chambermaid to say she was ill and wouldn't be able to make it. So I went in and worked for her as chambermaid and waitress. I had a marvelous time.

That was from the beginning of January until May. I had to work in the morning and do the rooms and had to wait on table and do the dishes and the rest of the time was free. I went out with the guests, a lot of whom I knew, and it was marvelous.

One thing which impressed me was that she was at home with any type of person; the party who drank in the morning and the people who were teetotallers. She just fitted in with anybody. She had a tremendous background. One day she said, "My grandmother entertained Caruso," and just took it for granted.

I always remember in the evenings we sometimes went out and skied by moonlight.

She would sit with her feet up on the stove and she would be writing her letters and answering her correspondence and she would crumple everything up and throw it on the floor. When she was finished she would gather it all up and throw it in the fire. I have always done that ever since. It is the greatest feeling when you are finished to pick it up and throw it away.

She studied "Snow Structure and Ski Fields." She called that her Bible because she was responsible for anyone who went out. She was great to go out with. She knew the birds. . . .

In the winter all I could do was the snow plow, but I went up Merlin Ridge and up the top of Douglas Glacier twice.

Everybody liked her. Bill Black, the warden, he and his wife Dorothy would always drop in — usually at tea time — and have tea.

She always greeted people with a cup of tea or something hot to drink when they arrived. Tea was always served in the afternoon when they came in. I know whenever anybody arrived they were always greeted. Anyone who came was welcome.

She always said that she wanted my husband and I to go into Skoki and stay at her expense, but we never did. She said we would have a cabin. We couldn't do that.

Jean (Vallance) Gill

*   *   *

Once, in early July, Lizzie had to go to Calgary to get a cook, so she asked me if I would look after things. Ila LaCasse was there. Elizabeth said, "If you can find time try and sit at the table with the people."

There were not too many people. There was a Dr. Mills from Hollywood who always wanted someone to go with him whenever he went some place. So I took him. I even took him to the top of Ptarmigan Mountain because he wanted to get into the Alpine Club. He lost his glasses, so I had to lend him my glasses. Finally he left and a week or so after I was going into Assiniboine and here was the doctor. When we got to Halfway Cabin I was getting supper ready. Finally he couldn't stand it any longer and he said to me.

"When you were at Skoki were you a guest or staff?"

"I don't know what I was at Skoki, but now there is no doubt about it, I am staff."

That was the end of it. He hardly looked at me after that. He wasn't a bit popular at Assiniboine so I didn't feel too bad.

When Lizzie brought in the cook she was a great big woman. They got her on a horse, but women didn't wear slacks then as they do now, so someone got a shawl which was wound around the saddle to protect her dignity.

It was lots of fun anyway. With all her difficulties Lizzie really liked it, but there really was an awful lot of really hard work.

The Coombs people came to Skoki once. He is the man who set up the German financial thing after the war. World wide financier. His wife was a psychiatrist.

Usually guests were given their lunch in a bag and they stayed out to lunch. However, this man wanted to come back to the lodge for lunch. I decided I would just give them what was left over from before, so I made a leftovers' casserole. The man raved about the casserole and asked for the recipe. I did that every day. No matter how I fixed it they always raved about it. Finally I told them what I did. They told me that at home they had a woman who came in and she had three things which she made and she just alternated those three things and they were never any different. You always know what you are going to get exactly.

At that time help was hard to get, so they were anxious to keep her. They enjoyed getting something different every day.

Muriel Gratz

*   *   *

People of every description and vocation went to Skoki Lodge and each left their mark on Lizzie's life and also in her guest book.

Snow squalls, intermittent sun. Skoki Peak with Elizabeth and Maudie.

Food like this takes not only art, but genius!

Deception didn't deceive us. It's as far up as down!

Heaven on earth!

Oh for another ten days.

Great fishing. What a walk! Oh my back!

What a lovely place for peace and inspiration.

Came in the rain but not singing.

Breath coming in short pants.

Back again after fourteen years. There is only one Skoki.

Should've eaten wheaties!

Someone forgot to switch the fan off on the top of the Pass. . . .

Many thanks to a perfect hostess.

Every time I come I make my dream materialize.

Ptarmigan Glacier by the left way (icefall) stopped before the top by cravasses. Excellent powder.

Douglas Glacier. Plenty of perfect powder snow. Glacier very good.

Merlin Ridge inconsistent snow and very rocky.

Mount Skoki top to timberline, excellent powder.

Mount Drummond north peak. Splendid downhill of 4,000 foot drop.

Elizabeth going out to ski with us in the morn.

Climb Skoki for a grand view but use rubber soled shoes or hobnails and <u>don't</u> turn right coming down as we did and wound up two miles from the lodge.

A perfect place. We shall return to griddle troots in the burn.

*Whose leg is he pulling? There must have been a twinkle in his eye when he said that!

*Timberline Tales, Jim Deegan, John Porter, The Peter Whyte Foundation, Banff, 1977.

CHAPTER IX

Another Trip To Europe

BY 1947 LIZZIE WAS MANAGING TEMPLE CHALET AND THE LAKE Louise Ski lodge as well as Skoki Lodge. The added responsibility meant she dealt with a larger staff and larger problems. The problem of the water system at Temple Chalet was a constant headache in the winter and the isolated situation of Skoki and Temple lodges created problems of their own which had to be constantly met. By the time the summer of 1949 drew to a close, Lizzie felt she was riding on the edge of her ability in the management of the three lodges. The problems involved with the management convinced Lizzie that it was time to get out of the situation and look for a place of her own which would be more suitable to her skills.

When the last guest left Skoki Lodge in September, so did Lizzie. She was tired but not defeated. Her dream of having a place of her own was still in her mind. With this dream in mind Lizzie and Muriel Gratz took a week's hiking holiday not far from Lake Louise, with two of Ray Legace's packhorses to carry their gear.

Setting out from Lake Louise, the two women hiked to the alpine meadows at Red Deer Lakes, down the Little Pipestone River, up Molar Creek and over the meadows of Molar Pass to Mosquito Creek and thence to the Banff-Jasper Highway.

> *Lizzie was really kind of thinking of a place to have a lodge.*
> *She was really looking things over. She never had any time*
> *in the summer to herself while at Skoki.*
>
> *Muriel Gratz*

During their holiday, the women camped at Baker Lake in a "not too wonderful tent." In the night a porcupine gnawed on the ridgepole of the tent and it was not long before the tent came down on top of the women. Muriel got out and chased the porcupine with a stick, while Lizzie hollered, "Don't you dare hurt that porcupine!" Muriel was all for lambasting the thing. Fortunately, it never came back.

At Red Deer Lakes the women visited the warden in the Cyclone wardens' cabin and were treated to tea. Lizzie knew the warden well due to the cabin's close proximity to Skoki Lodge.

It was a beautiful holiday for the two friends as well as a restful one for Lizzie.

After this scouting holiday, the women went on a week's climbing holiday in Glacier National Park in British Columbia, with Emile Cote as their guide. Here they climbed every day, except for the day it rained. The women put up with Cote's eccentricity of not climbing a peak unless he could be on top by noon.

Mounts Eagle and Tupper were among the peaks climbed. The party lodged in the Alpine Club of Canada's Hermit Hut and Wheeler Hut. Due to her facility in French, Lizzie got along famously with Cote, who could speak very little English.

"We really enjoyed that week," Muriel said later.

The following winter Lizzie spent most of her time between the home ranch and McLeod's boarding house and made plans for her future. Then on February 20th, leaving her plans in abeyance, Lizzie left Canada for a three month trip to Europe to visit her father and other relatives. Of the three trips which Lizzie made to Europe this is the one we know the most about as she very carefully kept a delightful diary of her activities.

Lizzie flew from Calgary, Alberta, first landing in Montreal, Quebec, where she stayed for two days visiting friends. From Montreal she flew to London, England. In London she met with Sir Norman Watson, with whom she always got along well, and discussed the Ski Club of the Canadian Rockies and its future.

Lizzie had a friend, Marion, in London with whom she frequently visited and shopped, but she also knew and met other people.

In early March, the Baroness Elizabeth von Rummel had lunch in the Connaught Hotel with Madame de Rosales, Marchesa Lady Salter and Sir Arthur Salter (MP for Oxford University), as well as having tea with Countess Blucher and an unknown princess.

"Like people that you read about," Lizzie of the Canadian Rocky Mountains, remarked in her diary.

Lizzie enjoyed her stay and the walks she had in St. James Park and the City of London.

From London Lizzie took a train to Scotland and Gordonstoun School where her step-aunt Traudl lived with her family. Traudl (a daughter of Georg Hirth's second marriage) had married a Jewish man named Victor Saloschin. They had left Germany shortly before the Second World War because of the anti-Jewish feelings and had relocated in Scotland. At Gordonstoun School Traudl and Victor taught riding and their excellent training is seen in the superb horsemanship of Prince Philip, the Duke of Edinburgh.

In the beautiful setting of Gordonstoun School, Lizzie visited for five days, watching the horses, touring the school, lunching with the head master, and sightseeing in the area with her aunt. For Lizzie, it was a nostalgic time as well. She and Traudl browsed through old photographs and talked of the days when they both lived in Germany.

Lizzie was thrilled with her visit to Gordonstoun School. Although she had grown up in the midst of culture, she had been away from cultural things for a long time. Watching the boys perform Highland dances and visiting the local priory, helped Lizzie to readjust to cultural life after lugging huge packs over Deception Pass and dealing with Temple Chalet's temperamental water system. The ranch girl in Lizzie, however, was not dormant as she gazed at long haired sheep and had the joy of seeing Clydesdale horses again.

Lizzie's insatiable curiosity was still evident as well. The night she left Gordonstoun School, on the train back to London, she read the history of the school far into the night. The conductor very kindly brought her tea at midnight, but welcome as it was, it could never assuage her thirst for knowing.

Arriving in London the next morning, Lizzie settled into a hotel before going to St. James Park with her friend Marion to watch a parade featuring King George VI and Queen Elizabeth.

While in London, Lizzie participated in several of London's cultural activities. She saw Margot Fontayne in Giselle at Covent Garden, a lovely Italian movie "Bitter Rice," at the Rialto Theatre, and visited Westminster Abbey, Big Ben, the embankment all along Millbank and the Tate Gallery. In the gallery she "saw all the familiar pictures" from her childhood of "Picasso, Utrillo, Braque, Matisse, Chajall, Gris, Van Gogh Gaugin and Rosetti." At Albert Hall she "heard beautiful music" and "was spellbound by the orchestra and choral singers." Later she wrote in her diary: "Felt elated over all what I saw and heard."

Lizzie met again Mr. Thomson, Sir Norman Watson's friend, in the Royal Automobile Club and talked of the Ski Club of the Canadian Rockies with him. She also met Hans-Peter, Traudl's son who had changed his name to Peter Saunders. Saunders had his own couture business and Lizzie visited a Home Exhibition where the furniture was upholstered with the material Saunders had designed. Lizzie felt Peter had "developed into a nice person."

After four days in London Lizzie flew to Vienna with a stop-over in Munich overnight due to a bad storm. This was Lizzie's first impression of Europe since World War II and the many "badly bombed sections" of Munich and Vienna filled her with sadness. In spite of the ravages of war around her, Lizzie had a wonderful eighteen day visit with her father, Gustav von Rummel, and his wife, Hertha (My) von Hagen.

Haus Hirth, Grainau.

> Papa and My. So pleasant and gemuthlich. They still have their old Marie. Then for dinner Frau Kathe Dorsch, actress and her secretary came. Good dinner and wine. Papa and My look very well. Interesting to listen to their conversation all about theatre, etc. They have small flat, some of their nice old things. I felt very happy.

Gustav von Rummel was now seventy-nine years old, but he was still active and interested in theatre productions, acting in minor roles and attending the theatre frequently. He and his wife took Lizzie to a wide variety of plays, including Antonia, Kluns Haus and Richard II, as well as operas and ballets. The theatre was usually followed by dinner in "pleasant and gemuthlich" Vienna restaurants. Everywhere they went together Lizzie was recognized as Gustav Waldau's (von Rummel's stage name) daughter and he was beseiged by autograph seekers.

As well as participating in the theatrical life of Vienna, Lizzie toured the city and its wonderful attractions, including many churches, a wide variety of shops (Stuben furniture was particularly appealing), several sites where famous people had lived and art galleries.

From Vienna Lizzie flew to Munich where she had many relatives. She was immediately aware of the difference between Munich and Vienna by the church steeples. She was also appalled by the devastation the war had wrought but, at the same time, impressed by the wonderful spirit of the people.

Leaving Munich for a couple of days, Lizzie had the great thrill to "at last pack a rucksack again" to go skiing with her cousin Medi in the mountains. While Medi returned to Munich, Lizzie stayed overnight in a mountain hut and the next day skied across country to where Medi and her husband, Hans, were competing in skiing competitions.

Back in Munich Lizzie visited scenes of her earliest childhood which brought back many memories and visited relatives in Munich and Rottach. Her step-aunt Louisl, sister to Traudl of Scotland, lived in Rottach and Lizzie and Louisl were very close friends. Years later Louisl visited Lizzie and her sister Jane in Canada.

On April 9th, Easter Sunday, Lizzie left Munich for Oberammergau where the men had already grown long hair in preparation for the famous Oberammergau festival and passion play.

> All men had already long hair, young boys and little children looked like angels. I went with Hans and Kathe on their yearly Osterspraziergang over meadows to a bench. Hans read the "Osterspaziergang" out of Faust, then we had lunch in their house. Babette, old maid with them for 47 years, remembers us as the "Weinmann Kinder." Went to hotel for rest. 5 p.m. we all went for walk through village. Preparations being made everywhere. Shops with carvings, tiny angels and pottery. Reminded me of Banff. Lovely setting, the village and mountains all around. Hans' house for supper. Very cosy.

While Lizzie was in Oberammergau a gentleman, Herr Nroink, came to Hans and Kathe's where Lizzie was staying and visited. They talked of the festival play and the tourist business.

> He brought a book of the history of guests who had been here. Grandfather Hirth signed and Gustav Waldau and he asked me to sign too.

Apparently, the Ski Club of the Canadian Rockies had a project in mind — expanding into lift skiing. Periodically Lizzie would discuss the project with her various relatives and other people with whom she came in contact. During an evening in Grainau, with relatives and others, she again talked about The Ski Club of the Canadian Rockies.

. . . .Late in evening suddenly conversation with all of them about S.C.C.R. project. Herr Aldag quite interested. Gave advice re lift. Found extremely quick conception and understanding and business knowledge and immense integrity in Herr Aldag.

It was while Lizzie was in Grainau that she wrote to Sir Norman Watson in England and invited him to look at the ski situation in Germany. Sir Norman, however, did not visit Grainau.

Lizzie went to Berwang on March 2nd. In this small pleasant village where she had been on holiday as a child with her mother and two sisters almost forty years before, Lizzie was amazed to find everyone remembered her and "asked after Hanni, Nina and Mother."

Ate with Victor's family. They have nine head of lovely grey cattle. The whole village is one smell of cow manure as now is the time they put it on the meadows. One side of the valley is all green, the other still snow with terrble snow slides still coming down. Slept in guest house which Koch's have. Valley and village give impression of high up and severe. I love that. Crocuses on meadows right against the snow.

While in Berwang, Lizzie went to see the burgermeister of the village as her mother still owned land in the village. Lizzie had to renegotiate the lease agreement for the land.

Went up to Grundstuck. House all gone. Piece of ground bigger than I thought — about two acres. Beautiful view. Remembered every stone, nothing changed except new hotels in village. Looked at altar in church, very lovely.

Lizzie stayed three days in Berwang and left "that country of our youth" with a feeling of sadness. From Berwang she went back to Grainau and her Uncle Walther and Tante Johanna's house until early May.

Beautiful warm sunny morning. Said goodbye to mountains, lovely house and garden. . . . .Tante Johanna and Walther went to Garmisch with me. Johanna said such dear things. Munich.

In Munich the family gave Lizzie a goodbye party on May 9th, with lots of wine and conversation. Lizzie did not get to bed until four in the morning, but said it was a "beautiful finish." The next day she caught the Orient Express. Tante Johanna accompanied her to the train where they met Lizzie's father, My and Frau Basil for lunch. Others came to see her off on the train which took her to the airport, from whence she flew to London, England.

Arriving in London, Lizzie was met by her friends Marion and Reg with whom she stayed overnight. On the twelfth she went to see Sir Norman Watson and later that day was taken to his estate, Haslemere, by chauffeur, for an interesting few days with Sir Norman and his guests.

At Haslemere, Lizzie walked in the garden among the bluebells, azaleas and rhododendrons, had lunch with Allan Campbell-Ord, a director of British Overseas Airways whom Lizzie had met at Temple Chalet, and Miss Hambling "a nice clever woman." Lizzie also had discussions about the Ski Club of the Canadian Rockies with Sir Norman and a Mr. Jolliff, but they reached an "unhappy deadlock."

We can only surmise, at this point, what might have been going on, but it seems to be something to do with developing lift skiing at Lake Louise in Canada.

From Abesters Farm at Haslemere Lizzie returned to London. Once again visiting with her friends Marion and Reg and also going on walks through Green Park, Hyde Park, Constitution Hill, the Mall and Pall Mall. She also visited other friends, attended a play, a film, and luncheoned with Marion at the Canadian Women's Club in order to hear a speech by Lord Tweedsmuir.

Marion took Lizzie to the airport on May 19th and, at three in the afternoon, she left London for Canada via Prestwick, Scotland, and Keflavik, Iceland (where she had tea), landing in Sidney, Nova Scotia (where she had coffee).

Wonderful this flying in the sky. Stars above and below, the plane a bluish grey, greenish colour, the engines showing red hot, fantastic unearthly light.

Arriving in Montreal at seven in the morning Lizzie took a room at the Mount Royal Hotel and in the afternoon went to see Miss Doyle and Mr. Lippsman regarding Sir Norman Watson's Ski Club of the Canadian Rockies project, but found Mr. Lippsman was "no good to us."

On the 21st she flew to Ottawa, then Toronto, where she was met by her friends the Grierson family, with whom she stayed. One of Lizzie's first impressions on her return to Canada was how prosperous, clean and bright Canada appeared. While in Toronto the Grierson family threw a party for Lizzie and showed films of Skoki. Many of the Skoki Lodge guests had come from Toronto, including the Griersons. Mr. and Mrs. Grierson entertained Lizzie for several days, taking her to St. Catharines to visit their daughter and their place at Annadale. Lizzie particularly enjoyed the beautiful flowering shrubs and trees in the orchard which was situated on the edge of a wild ravine and, as always, she enjoyed meeting new people and seeing new places.

Leaving Toronto on a late night flight, Lizzie arrived in Calgary at seven in the morning and had a happy reunion with her family from the ranch and her mother, who came from Banff. This marked the "finish of three wonderful months" which would benefit Lizzie in the next adventure she embarked upon.

CHAPTER X

Sunburst Lake Camp

LIZZIE'S TRIP TO EUROPE PREPARED HER FOR HER NEW ROLE IN LIFE. The cultural aspect of her life in Europe as a child was viewed in an entirely different way than the cultural experiences she absorbed on this momentous trip in 1950. The effects of this holiday cannot be over-emphasized. Why Lizzie was so involved in discussions about the future of the Ski Club of the Canadian Rockies while in Europe is uncertain. Sir Norman Watson was apparently including Lizzie in his plans for the S.C.C.R., but what that inclusion consisted of is very unclear. Whatever their mutual plans were, they were all blown to the winds the day Lizzie met Pat Brewster on the streets of Banff.

Pat Brewster had offered to sell his cabin on the shore of Sunburst Lake at Mount Assiniboine to Erling Strom. Strom wasn't interested in buying the cabin but said possibly Lizzie Rummel would be. Not long afterwards Lizzie met Brewster on the street in front of the Mount Royal Hotel in Banff. The first thing Brewster blurted out was, "Would you like to buy Sunburst Lake, my cabin there?"

Lizzie was taken aback with surprise as she had always thought Pat would want it for the Brewster family.

"No, no, I want you to have it," Pat said emphatically.

"Is it still there?" Lizzie had not seen the cabin for nearly ten years.

"Yes, I think so."

Although Lizzie had spent all her money on her trip to Europe, she was determined to have Sunburst Cabin, so in order to secure the two thousand dollars required to purchase the cabin, she sold her life insurance policy and all her cattle from the ranch. This sale not only gave her the purchase price of the cabin, but some capital with which to start a business.

On December 2nd, 1950, the Agreement for Sale was signed and Sunburst Camp was Lizzie's.

In my wildest dreams I never dreamt I would own that little cabin.

Sunburst Lake Camp, situated at an elevation of 2,190 meters, had been built by George Thurber and Johnny Boychuk about 1934 or 1935 for Pat Brewster. The logs had been felled from behind the cabin, in the direction of Cerulean Lake, and the cabin built on the shore of Sunburst Lake was nestled in the trees but gave an excellent view of Sunburst Peak and Mount Assiniboine. The cabin was about four meters wide and five and a half meters long. Lizzie, of course, had seen Sunburst Cabin many times when she was working for Strom at his Mount Assiniboine Lodge on the edge of Magog Lake, no more than two kilometers away.

While Lizzie's joy on acquiring the cabin knew no bounds, her friends were horrified that Lizzie, almost fifty-four years old, was prepared to start over again in the risky mountain lodge business. Every one of her friends told her she was crazy and a fool. That didn't matter to Lizzie. She went ahead and made her plans and had her dreams until February of 1951. At that time she couldn't stand the suspense any longer and just had to go into Mount Assiniboine and see the cabin.

February 28th saw Al Gaetz and Lizzie flying over the mountains from Banff to Mount Assiniboine. Gaetz landed his Piper Cruiser plane on Magog Lake where he and Lizzie unloaded their packs and skis in the shadow of snowclad Mount Assiniboine. From the lake they skied through the deep powder snow, up a little cooley towards Sunburst Lake, in what Lizzie hoped was the right direction. After ten years it was hard to remember the right way but as the cooley narrowed they headed into the trees, across small sunlit snowy meadows to Sunburst Lake. At the lake they skied along the lakeshore until they saw a big mushroom. Hidden under several meters of snow the cabin did look like a mushroom. Al managed to clamber through the snow onto the roof and get the tin off the chimney pipe, while Lizzie scrambled down the snowbank and put her key into the padlock on the door.

We. . . .was wonderful. . . .opened the door, I had the key, went in and there was a little tiny packers' stove.

Al and Lizzie opened the shutters on the windows and found the south window had no pane. Al found an old piece of carpet lying

Lizzie and Mt. Assiniboine. 1952.

around and nailed it over the window. The logs of the cabin were desperately in need of chinking, but Lizzie was not disheartened.

> I would not have given it up for a million dollars. It was just one big adventure.

Lizzie skied back to the plane on Magog Lake with Al as she had another load of gear to carry to the cabin.

> I stood on that lake and saw him fly off, and there I was. That was one of the biggest moments in my life. And now I said, "It's up to me. I am going to prove I can do it." If I couldn't do it I would have got no sympathy. They would all have said "We told you so." I put my sleeping bag on my back and I skied back up and I made a fire and melted some snow. It was so cold in that cabin if I dropped water on that table it would have froze right away. I had said to Al, "Supposing I freeze to death in here?" He said, "No,

you've got that arctic sleeping bag and it's suppose to stand thirty below." And then he said, "I'll come back in three days and fly you out again." I never took my parka off. I had a real good sleep that night in my good sleeping bag. I had bread, butter and raisins and in the daytime I went out and got loose branches off the trees for firewood. I made many trips. The little bit of firewood which was in the cabin was not enough. It was lovely weather. Al did chop down an old tree before he left. He came back in three days and buzzed the cabin, so I skied down to the lake.

When Al returned, he brought more supplies and cabin gear which he and Lizzie hauled to the cabin in their packs. They then closed up the cabin, locking the door, closing the shutters on the windows and putting the tin on the stove pipe to keep the snow out. Once the cabin was closed Lizzie and Al skied back to Magog Lake and boarded the small Piper Cruiser plane for the flight back to Banff.

In Banff Lizzie convinced Aileen Harmon, Muriel Gratz and Irene Reader to go into the cabin with her for the Easter holiday week.

I don't know what's going to happen, but we'll live through it.

Being adventuresses themselves, the three women consented to go with Lizzie. Subsequently, on March 26th, Lizzie and Aileen flew to Mount Assiniboine with Al Gaetz, followed by Muriel and Irene the next day. The women immediately set about chinking logs and fetching firewood.

The following day Al Gaetz returned with a better cookstove and skied with the girls to the Alpine Club huts (now the Naiset Cabins) and borrowed the Club toboggan to haul the stove up to Sunburst Cabin. Al helped install the stove before flying back to Banff.

Muriel, Irene and Aileen had gone together and bought Lizzie a pressure cooker because they thought it would be good at high altitudes and save on fuel. None of the women had used a pressure cooker before and were scared of it, but since some of the vegetables had frozen Aileen threw them all in the pot with a ham bone and proceeded to make soup. The other women, not trusting the pressure cooker, stood at the door of the cabin ready to bolt should the cooker blow up.

The cooker didn't blow up and the soup surprised everyone by turning out to be "the best soup you had ever tasted in your life."

Surviving the soup, log chinking and the good skiing, Aileen flew out to Banff with Gaetz on the thirty-first and Muriel and Irene followed on the first of April.

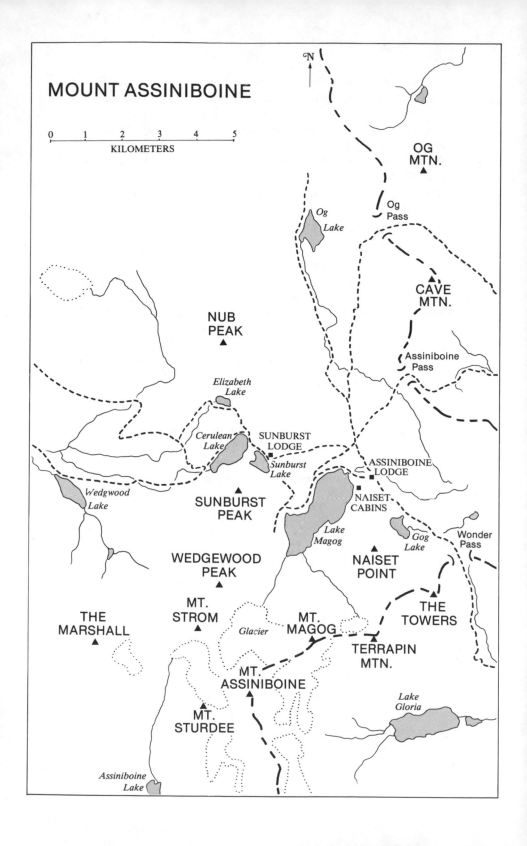

A lovely Easter holiday for us four girls, good skiing and good company. Six full days.

While the three women went back to their jobs in Banff, Lizzie stayed at Sunburst and prepared for her first official guests who arrived on April 3rd. Two of the guests came from New York and two from Quebec. They stayed four days and enjoyed the skiing immensely.

It is not hard to enjoy the skiing at Mount Assiniboine as the area has some of the best ski touring in the Canadian Rocky Mountains. Meadows, lakes, benchlands, as well as mountains, always with superb and dramatic views, give the skier a feeling of being on top of the world.

The day after Lizzie's first guests left, Jean Sanderson, from Calgary, flew in alone with Al Gaetz. Al was in a hurry so he quickly unloaded Jean's ski outfit on Magog Lake and said, "Well, so long for now. You'll find Elizabeth's cabin over in that direction."

Suddenly I found myself alone. I put on my seal skins, strapped on my pack and followed some blown over ski tracks and hoped I find the cabin — I did — also found my ever charming friend and hostess.

Jean stayed four days, leaving Lizzie with a feeling of a "nice and congenial visit."

Shortly after Jean left Erling Strom brought a party of four into his Mount Assiniboine Lodge on the edge of Magog Lake. Lizzie skied over and visited them and invited them to a delightful dinner at her cabin. Three days later she skied to Banff with Strom's party, over Assiniboine and Allenby passes and down Brewster Creek, staying at Strom's Halfway Cabin enroute.

That was the beginning.

The beginning of "twenty beautiful years" . . . . and hard work, and pain, and laughter and hundreds of new and lasting friendships.

CHAPTER XI

Lizzie Finds Her Forté

FROM THIS MODEST BEGINNING OF SPRING SKIING, LIZZIE LAUNCHED into the summer tourist camp business in early July. She immediately secured the services of Ray McBride of Canmore, as her summer outfitter, to haul supplies into Sunburst Lake.

McBride would drive up the Spray Valley, from Canmore, to Turbulent Creek, where he kept his horses corralled and thence ride his pack outfit into Mount Assiniboine, a distance of thirty kilometers. Lizzie would send messages for new supplies to McBride via Strom's riders who regularly went to Banff. McBride then picked up the camp bookings from Jean Waterhouse in Banff, and the necessary supplies in Canmore, loaded it all into pack boxes and onto his packhorses and rode into Lizzie's camp at Sunburst Lake.

At the beginning of the season Lizzie had the summer's supply of dry goods brought into the camp via one packtrain, but fresh vegetables and meat had to be packed in by horse once a week. McBride acted as outfitter to Lizzie for the duration of her operation of Sunburst Camp.

While McBride acted as outfitter, Jean (formerly McLeod) Waterhouse acted as booking agent. She too worked with Lizzie the whole time Lizzie operated the camp.

Jean and Lizzie had been friends since Lizzie first went to Banff in 1938 and stayed in the McLeod boarding house. Later Jean married Hal Waterhouse, an R.C.M.P. officer, and had three children. In November of 1951 Waterhouse died very suddenly of a heart attack. It was after Hal's death that Lizzie moved into the big house in Banff with Jean, when she was not at Sunburst Camp. Lizzie lived with Jean for the eight years Jean was a widow. When Jean remarried, Lizzie moved into a small, draughty, log cabin on the edge of the Bow River.

Jean knew about advertising for the tourist business since she had

Lizzie's tipi and one of the tent-frame cabins.

worked for her father in the Rocky Mountain Tours company, hence she was a valuable asset to Lizzie. Between them they designed little folders to advertise Sunburst Camp and deposited them in the information booths in Banff. Jean would keep one booking book in her house in Banff and Lizzie kept another at Sunburst Camp. Between them they always knew exactly how many people could be accommodated. Once or twice a mistake was made but somehow Lizzie always managed.

To keep Lizzie informed of new bookings or other events, Jean would send little notes with Ray McBride to Assiniboine. Often these notes would say whether or not Jean felt the people would enjoy Assiniboine, or if they would be a problem. When Lizzie came into Banff in the fall she always said, "Boy, you hit them all right again this year!"

For the nineteen summers Jean looked after Lizzie's bookings she never took any money. She did it because she loved Lizzie and enjoyed the work.

Initially Lizzie had three tent-frame cabins. Later a fourth was set up in the back meadow. A little wooden cabin, behind the main cabin, was built by Charlie Hunter and her sister Jane. This cabin was to be used by Lizzie and her helper but usually accommodated guests and Lizzie and her helper slept in the main cabin. Many times this small cabin was given to honeymooners. Kent Shaefer, who often went to Sunburst Camp with his friends, brought his bride Maida on their honeymoon and Lizzie gave them the little cabin. She also did not charge them for their accommodation, just for the food. "A wonderful wedding present."

Each spring the tent frames had to be cleaned out and set up. Ken Jones often helped set up tents. The wooden frame wall was about three feet high, with a wood floor. The tent touched on the edge of the wall, tied on with nails and hooks. The two single beds in each cabin had spring mattresses and were metal frame construction. An airtight heater sat at the foot of the bed with a box for wood nearby. A shelf supported enamel basins and soap dishes. Between the beds there was a piece of wood on which to sit a coal oil lamp or a little candle. A cowhide rug from the ranch lay on the floor between the beds, adding a finishing touch to the rustic decor.

Every morning when Lizzie arose, she would light the kitchen stove and put the kettle on; then she, or her helper, would go into the guests' cabins and light a fire in the little airtight heaters at the foot of the beds. The guests loved this "roughing it deluxe" mountain life. Lying in their beds they would listen to the rain on the tent roof or be wakened by the heat of the morning sun. The crackling fire took the chill out of the tent and warmed the wash water.

The main cabin had two single cots, each along a wall, which were used as couches during the day, a wood burning stove, cupboards, shelves, the long dining table and benches. On the rafters above Lizzie stored her flour, oatmeal and other dried goods out of the way of mice. As well, there was a small supply tent erected behind this main cabin in which most of the canned goods, potatoes, onions and carrots were stored on wooden frames. The fresh meat was kept in a tin-lined box wedged into a hole in the ground near the lake. The lake kept the meat box cool and never seemed to attract wild animals.

In front of the main cabin was a hitching rail. Lizzie also had a large tipi in the middle of which a fire burned brightly in the evenings and many sing songs were washed down with hot chocolate and conversation. The camp held eight to ten guests at the most.

Lizzie's excellent cooking and personal charm endeared everyone to her. She always knew when a cup of tea was in order, particularly after a long day on the trail. During her last years at the camp, when she

Harry Green and Lizzie at Sunburst Cabin.

was more crippled with arthritis, she was always glad when people came by as she loved meeting new people and seeing old friends.

Lizzie also revelled in having her sisters and their families visit her at Sunburst Camp. Every year Nina and Paddy Rodgers tried to go into the camp at the beginning of the season to help her set up the tents. Nina and Paddy usually went into the camp by horse, but Jane, an avid hiker, always walked. The last summer Lizzie operated the camp Jane walked the eighteen kilometers from Spray Lake to Sunburst Lake, at the age of seventy-two.

At first Lizzie did all the work herself, but by 1955, if not earlier, she had hired a girl to help her in the heavier work. In the nineteen summers in which she operated the camp there were only five or six girls who worked for her. Liana Van Der Bellen, a young girl who had escaped from Estonia with her family as a child, and about whom another book could be written, worked for Lizzie at least six summers for a month each summer. Liana was going to McGill University in Montreal at the time. Myrna Collins, now Myrna Frank and living in Switzerland, worked for Lizzie for six summers as well.

If you are nervous, neurotic, or dyspeptic come and try it for a week or two. The cure is certain.

Liana Van Der Bellan
Montreal, Québec

My deepest wish is to be here next year at "Lizzie's Place" — the person and the place are inseparable.

Myrna Collins
Dawson Creek and
Prince George, B.C.

Ruth Wilson and Lizzie inside Sunburst Cabin.

Lizzie, I haven't words to thank you for thirty-nine most tremendous days of happiness working together. As far as I am concerned, it's been just one big, fabulous holiday. I'll miss you very much.

God fashioned many flowers rare which to us he lends,
But the sweetest from his garden fair
Are those he labelled — FRIENDS!

Lil Notland
Banff, Alberta

. . . .It is part of my life to be here. . . .

Ruth Wilson
Canmore, Alberta

Sunburst Lake Camp guest book.

As well as the female help which Lizzie used in running the Sunburst Camp, she also had two good male friends without whom she could not have managed. One was Ken Jones, mentioned earlier, and the other was Charlie Hunter.

Charlie was a retired farmer and packer, who spent many summers in the Mount Assiniboine area, accompanied by his saddle horse and packhorse. Ken usually came into Assiniboine to help Lizzie in the fall of each year. He cut wood for the following year and did many odd jobs around the camp. In the spring of 1952 he and Michael Vosper roofed the main cabin. Vosper was a tough, little Cornishman who could speak about ten languages and Jones was an equally tough, lanky Canadian.

Jones was a man of many talents and jobs in the mountains. Bridget, his wife, once said, "Regular is not a word that applies to Ken." Not only did Jones cook for camps, but he also built log buildings in the mountains, including Num-ti-jah Lodge at Bow Lake north of Lake Louise. In 1966 or 1967 he became the first ranger to reside in Mount Assiniboine Provincial Park (which encompassed Lizzie's and Strom's camps) and remained in that capacity, during the summer months, for seven years.

Charlie Hunter first met Lizzie when she was at Skoki Lodge and he was taking a party up Mount Richardson. He had taken Lizzie along on the climb. He met her again at Mount Assiniboine. Charlie became very fond of Lizzie and spent many years chopping wood, erecting tents and hauling water for her at Sunburst Camp.

*   *   *

I always helped Lizzie as much as I possibly could. She had a hard deal. Fate was terrible to Lizzie. That illness she got which crippled her up so much just ruined her life. I always felt sorry for Lizzie and helped her in every way I possibly could, but without pay. I

69

would split wood and set up tents and take down tents and do odd jobs. Anything that she would find hard to do herself.

Charlie Hunter

* * *

I was staying with Lizzie one time. We stayed up rather late as Lizzie had heard a porcupine the night before and she wanted me to chase it away. Finally I went to bed, in my tent nearby, but had not been in bed very long. I was just dozing off when Lizzie banged on the tent.

"Ken, Ken, there's a porky around."

I got my clothes on and found the porky alright so killed him by a tap on the nose with a pick handle. I had to watch the tail didn't swing around and hit me. I took the porcupine up by the woodpile and laid him out. The next morning I got up early to bury him before Lizzie got up. Instead of one out there, there were three dead porcupines laid out in the woodpile. Side by side. Just like pieces of wood.

"What in Sam hill is going on here?"

Anyway, I hauled the three porkys away and dug a big hole up behind some trees. By the time I hauled the third one away Lizzie must have been up and seen me but I was too busy to notice. When I came back to the cabin, smoke was coming out of the chimney. Lizzie said, "You'd better come, coffee's getting ready."

I must have had a puzzled look on my face when I said, "Where in hell did all those three porkys come from Lizzie? I only killed one last night."

She looked at me kind of sheepish.

"You know I didn't have the nerve to go and wake you again but as soon as you got rid of that one porky there was another one came along. So I grabbed the bottle of whiskey and took a couple of good slugs and went out there with that pick handle and lambasted hell out of him. I went and put it where you put the first one. I just got nicely in bed again and another one came around, so I took a couple more good slugs of whiskey and picked up the pick handle and lambasted that one. You know, that was an awful thing. Those poor things didn't do a thing."

She was feeling sorry for the porkys.

Ken Jones

* * *

Another man who became very important in Lizzie's life was Hans Gmoser. Gmoser is famous today for his helicopter skiing and heli-hiking in the British Columbia mountains. In 1952, however, Gmoser was a recent emigre to Canada and was "as poor as a church mouse."

Gmoser came into Lizzie's life at the time The Alpine Club of Canada was holding its annual camp at Mount Assiniboine. He wanted

70

Lizzie, Franz Dopf and Hans Gmoser at Sunburst Cabin.

to climb with the club but couldn't afford to stay in the club camp, so he erected a wicki-up in the bush nearby. Lizzie discovered him and took him under her wing, putting him up in her camp. During the next two winters Gmoser guided for Lizzie and was launched on a Canadian mountain career that has become world famous.

In many ways Lizzie was like a mother to Gmoser. Whenever he was at Assiniboine he would stay with her and often she would get up at two in the morning to make he and his friends breakfast before they set off on a climb. In turn, Gmoser helped Lizzie in whatever work was needed to be done in the camp. Lizzie always felt Gmoser was one of the best climbers she knew and she had tremendous faith in his ability. She watched his climbing career with avid interest and they remained close friends for the rest of her life.

In the summer of 1953 Lizzie and her guests kept a careful eye on Gmoser and Franz Dopf as they made the first ascent of Sunburst Wall — across Sunburst Lake from Lizzie's camp.

First ascent of Sunburst Peak NE face.
Height 1,500 ft. — 500 M.
Difficult Grade V.
Franz Dopf
Hans Gmoser
Linz, Austria.
Time: 5 hours.
Name of Route: "Elizabeth Route"

In Honor of Miss Elizabeth Rummel for her kind hospitality.
Sunburst Camp guest book.

One year Gmoser broke his leg, so Lizzie asked Jean Waterhouse
if she could put him up in her large house. Jean willingly complied.
Gmoser thus spent the winter with Lizzie and Jean while recovering
from his injury.

Lizzie was always very interested in young climbers. Throughout
her life she had many friends in the climbing world and most of them
were the best mountain climbers in Canada. As well as Gmoser,
Philippe DeLaSalle, Jim Willer, Joe Plaskett, Tak Tanabe and many
others enjoyed Lizzie's wonderful hospitality while they were climbing
or hiking in the mountains.

None of the young men whom Lizzie befriended could afford to
stay in her camp. (She was charging seven dollars a night, with meals).
Lizzie, however, put them up and did not ask for payment. In return the
fellows did odd jobs for her and gave her their affection. She often
referred to them as "my boys," and remained friends with all of them,
and subsequently with their wives, for the rest of her life.

Lizzie shared her love of Assiniboine with her boys and nourished
an appreciation of the mountains in their hearts. Once she quietly
called Jim Willer to her side and took him to a plateau above her cabin
where The Nub and Mount Assiniboine could be seen; sharing with
him one of her special places where she went in the evenings after her
work was finished.

         *   *   **

I met Lizzie at Sunburst, as I recall, in the presence of Hans
Gmoser, who had helped her at the cabin. It was in the shadow of her
friendship for Hans that I met her and since I was going through the
interesting and hard adjustment of working for Erling, whom I greatly
admired and loved as a father (My own father had died about four years
before and as is human, I had sought for another, and Erling was he.)
Erling was a man as critically atheistic and anti-clerical and anti-
Catholic (then) as I was simply Catholic, with a deep sense of God's
presence in nature.

Since I was going through such an adjustment, my meeting with
Lizzie was deep indeed, for in her, without much talk at all, I felt an
ally, a deep support. I didn't know how deep until a few years after I
entered the Jesuits and wrote to explain to her a little how the two
summers at Assiniboine (in its surroundings, in the fierce and yet solid
thrust of the mountain and in the lives of us working around its base) led
me to hear a call to choose to live along the lines of the best religious
order I knew then — the Jesuits.

She wrote a few lines, how once she had been walking in the upper end of the valley at Halfway Hut near Skoki, alone, and slowly entered such an intense presence of God's existence and holiness that she had no choice, no inclination to do anything but fall to her knees — not to "pray" or speak, but to recognize and worship, to be there, to acknowledge that the whole thing — the whole world — was in His care, in His design and protection.

Fr. Peter DuBrul

*   *   *

I first went to Assiniboine as a guest, on holiday from England. I went for two days and stayed two months. Erling said, "Well, you just stay and you won't pay me and I won't pay you and we'll get along fine." By the end of that time I knew Lizzie pretty well.

I went to Assiniboine in 1955 to work for Erling Strom. There was always a big staff at Erling's and sometimes there would be a raucus. The staff would go over to Lizzie's and she would calm their ruffled feathers. There was nowhere to go otherwise.

For Erling's birthday Lizzie always came over to Assiniboine Lodge. Usually later in the fall she would come over and they would have a good supper and everyone would get together.

Bridget Jones

*   *   *

The beginning years at Sunburst Camp were not easy years. There were insufficient guests to support Lizzie during the remainder

Christmas 1953 in Harry and Rene Burfields' cabin on Hollyburn Mountain. Photo courtesy of Catharine McDowell.

73

of the year and Lizzie, not one to be idle in any event, went to Vancouver, British Columbia, and worked for Ila LaCasse in the coffee shop at HiView Lodge on Hollyburn Mountain. Lizzie worked in the coffee shop the winters of 1953 and 1954; mainly behind the counter as a general dogs' body — washing dishes, making hamburgers, serving coffee, etcetera. The work was very arduous but was weekends only as it was not busy during the week.

Downhill skiing was just coming into vogue at this time, so the coffee shop clientelle mainly came from Vancouver and stayed in their own log cabins or came to ski for the day. It was a mixed bunch and everyone liked Lizzie but they were not really the kind of people with her love of the outdoors, although some were.

While working in the coffee shop, Lizzie lived in a cold, damp, log cabin which Ila rented for her. She fitted in with the community and regular residents on the mountain and they recognized her worth and loved her. Although there were a lot of drop-outs and ski bums, there were also a few genuine mountain people, such as the Burfields who ran Hollyburn Lodge, and Oscar Burson, the last of the three original Swedes who had built Hollyburn Lodge and who was also involved in building HiView Lodge.

In November of 1954 Lizzie and her friend Catharine McDowell went to Windermere, British Columbia, and stayed in Dr. Blair Fulton's cabin. Cathy went to paint and Lizzie to visit friends and enjoy the jaunt. The weather, however, became too cold for Cathy to paint outside so both took a job bundling up Christmas trees. Everyone in the Columbia Valley works at Christmas trees in November.

Lizzie enjoyed the hard work and the community feeling of working alongside the local people. When the weather improved Cathy went back to painting but Lizzie continued at the Christmas tree work. It was at this time that Cathy painted a picture of Lizzie working on the Christmas trees.

1954 was also the last year Lizzie ran her Sunburst Camp for spring skiing. Financially it was no longer worthwhile due to the advent of downhill skiing. There were not enough people interested in ski touring.

CHAPTER XII

Pain and Suffering

WHILE WORKING IN VANCOUVER LIZZIE WENT TO SEE A DR. PRESTON about the pain in her hip which had bothered her for some time. Dr. Preston diagnosed her problem as arthritis and began treating Lizzie for the ailment. By 1956 she had acquired a noticeable limp. That summer Dr. J. S. Gardner and Dr. Russell McManus, two Calgary surgeons, visited Sunburst Camp at Mount Assiniboine, at the insistence of a friend.

*   *   *

I was in the habit of going on little hikes, and I had a surgeon friend who was too busy and every once in a while he had to go somewhere. It was in the early part of the year and we were very busy at the hospital and we had a peak of really problem cases, so he said to me one day.

"If you are going for a walk, I want to go with you."

"I am not going for another walk until I can camp out about one night or two."

So this was fine and one day I went down to the Belcher Hospital. Lizzie's pet was Neil Brown who worked in the lab at the Belcher — we used to talk about what we were going to do in the outdoors. So I said I was going to go overnight with Dr. McManus.

Brown said, "You have to go where I am going to show you, to see Miss Lizzie Rummel."

"Well, how far is it?"

"You can drive thirty miles and walk fourteen."

"I am not going to walk fourteen miles. We are going to have huge packs with tents and we are going to go comfortably, and we can't walk fourteen miles."

75

"You've got to. You've simply got to. I want you to come and see me tomorrow morning."

The next morning when I saw him he said, "This is something you've got to do. I am going to hound you until you do this."

He had the map on which he had drawn the route with red arrows all the way to Sunburst Lake.

I said, "It looks like more than fourteen miles."

"It's only fourteen miles and I'll admit it is a little uphill and there is a pass to go over."

"Don't you realize we are working doctors and out of shape?"

"Well," he said, "then camp on the way. Go, you've got to meet Miss Rummel. I know her well and I know you well and you two have got to meet. Period."

"Well, what is she like?"

"Well, she comes from Germany and you'd love her right away and she would love you right away."

"Ah, come on, stop it. Nonsense."

"No, no, you've got to meet. You two have got to meet."

So, finally I spoke to Russ and told him and he said, "Well, let's try it."

So, we toiled and we toiled up that long, long. . . .what we thought was one hundred and fourteen miles, and we got to where we had to go up over the hill and he said, "I can't go."

"We'd better go and stay overnight and camp somewhere and then we can visit her tomorrow."

So we plodded over that hill and when we went down there was nobody in the cabin and there was nothing happening.

"We'd better. . . .this must be the cabin Neil told us about and it is certainly the lake and the whole bit. Let's just push off down here and put our tent up somewhere."

Whereupon a voice said, "Oh, hello, hello."

There was Liana Van Der Bellen and Lizzie pulling the old stove into the woods just to the lakeside of the cabin; putting it out of sight and they were both dishevelled and I think Lizzie's, and perhaps Liana's, hands were black. They had just polished the new stove and had been carrying the old stove.

Lizzie said, "We weren't going to say anything, we looked so terrible but you looked as though you were going away."

"Are you Miss Rummel?"

"Yes."

"Well, I'm Mr. Gardner."

"Oh."

"And this is Mr. McManus and we're camping out and is there a place where we could tent?"

"Oh well, over across the lake, or down there by the creek or so. You look awfully tired."

"We sure are tired. By the way, do people live in these tents?"

"Oh yes, but we haven't opened yet because it is too early in the season."

"What do you rent them for?"

"Eight dollars a night."

"What?"

"Would you like to stay?"

"I would love to stay. Could we?"

Well, we aren't very tidy yet."

"Is there a bed? Or a place for a bedroll on the floor?"

"You can stay overnight. We're in awful shape too you know. We've been cleaning up the cabin and moving stoves and so on."

"That doesn't matter. We're in awful shape too."

"Have you had your supper?" It was about seven-thirty or eight o'clock.

"No, but we have some cheese and bread. You don't make suppers do you?"

"Well, if you don't mind waiting until we clean up, we'll make you supper."

"Really! Would you?"

"Yeah. If you want to wait awhile. Go and put your things in the first cabin there and you can light a fire if it's cold and we'll shout when supper is made."

She had some canned meat, prem and some canned carrots and we went in and she was mixing up some stuff and she said, "Have you ever eaten powdered potatoes?"

"My goodness no; they must be good."

"No they aren't. They are terrible. I'll put a little milk and butter in this one for you, because you are so tired."

"Make lots."

"I have, a whole pot full."

Well, that was the best meal I ever ate in my life. So we went to bed and before we went she asked what we would like for breakfast.

"Well, anything. Whatever you have."

"Well, bacon and eggs and hot cakes and fruit and so on."

"Well, alright. We have stuff in our packs but your food is a lot better than we can make."

So we went to breakfast when they called us and that was the best breakfast in the whole world. Just as we were drinking our coffee —

and she had treated us as usual — casual — and she was running back and forth and she had a limp. So I said, "Oh, you hurt your leg?"

"Yes."

"It looks in your hip."

"Yes."

"I imagine you've got a little arthritis in your hip."

"How do you know that? You've never seen me before."

"No."

"Do you know Dr. Preston in Vancouver?"

"No, I don't know Dr. Preston anywhere. Why?"

"He's my doctor. He told me I had arthritis in my hip. How did you know?"

Then Russ burst out laughing. He said, "Well, Miss Rummel, he's a hip surgeon."

"I'll never forgive you for not telling me last night."

Liana said, "He's a surgeon!" Turning to Russ she said, "What are you?"

"I'm a surgeon too. He trained me."

Lizzie turned to me and said, "Why didn't you tell us last night?"

"We were busy and we were tired, and why should I?"

"Oh, I wish you had warned me you were surgeons."

"Just exactly what would you have done?"

"Oh, we would have been very much more careful."

"Thank God we didn't tell you."

We went fishing and I don't know how many Russ caught but I caught thirteen trout in the end of Magog Lake. There was a lot of snow around so I buried them in the snow until I caught them all and brought them back, and Lizzie said, "Oh, why did you catch so many?"

"Well, I like to fish."

"Oh, that's far too many isn't it and I hate cooking them."

"I'll cook them."

"No, no, a doctor can't cook fish."

"Yes, a doctor can."

"Now, are you married?"

"Yes, her name is Laura."

"Well, you're going to take those four big ones home to Laura."

"Look, I've got a huge pack and they are about two pounds each. That is eight more pounds you want me to carry out."

"Can't you?"

"No."

She took those four big fish out and buried them in the snow as we were going to stay one more night. They were absolutely frozen. The following morning, by the time we had our breakfast, she had them all wrapped up in newspaper so that they would come home to my family. By the time I got to the end of Spray Lake I hated every ounce of those fish. Oh my, they were heavy.

That was my first meeting with Lizzie.

Dr. J. S. (Smitty) Gardner

*   *   *

Sometime later a mutual friend arranged that Lizzie would go to Calgary and see Dr. Gardner about her arthritis.

> Sure enough, she did have bad arthritis in the one hip. I gave her some advice and may have given her some anti-arthritic pills. I really don't know how long she went on as a lot happened in the meantime.

Lizzie first met the Gardner family after she had been to see Dr. Gardner in his office. On one occasion she and her sister Jane had dinner with them. Although the Gardners did not see much of Lizzie over the next two years, they did go into Mount Assiniboine with their three children — Jim, Don and Mary Ann. At that time Lizzie had an arrangement with the rangers of the area, in which she could use the ranger's cabin near her camp. She gave the Gardner family this cabin and they looked after their own breakfasts and lunches, but had dinner with Lizzie and her guests in Lizzie's cookhouse.

*   *   *

We had only got to know her a short time when one day she announced: "Well, now I will take you to my special private picnic place."

"How could it be so special?"

"It's very special. I don't take anybody there. I just go myself and my very, very closest friends. I would take Nina or Janey."

So away we went as a family. Between Cerulean and Sunburst Lakes there is a valley where there used to be a stream and some knolls and as you go up on your right it gets thicker and you can't make your way through there, but if you go around Cerulean Lake you can make your way up the bank and then you can go over and it's an open spot and it is a knoll nearly flat and beautiful bushes, flowers and trees. It opens out and you get a beautiful view over Cerulean Lake and to the west, looking at all the western mountains. Lizzie knew this place and she saved it for very special people. When we got taken there she would mention, every once in awhile, that only the most special people got taken there.

There is a lot between when we first went into Assiniboine and her surgery. We used to go in every summer. After I had seen her once or twice. . . .and we didn't have medicare and I don't know whether we even had M.S.I., but for kindness I didn't charge her anything. I may have charged her ten dollars or something, I can't remember. But by the time we went in to stay, when it came to pay the bill, she said "You're not going to pay for your lodging. The food has to be carried in but the lodging is here and you're not going to pay for yours."

"Well, I won't come then."

"Well, I won't speak to you anymore then."

So it went; that I'd go in, she would make up the bill and every year this went on, and I'd add on what I thought would be the equivalent and say, "Now Lizzie you have to take this." As time went on I looked after her more and referred her to the proper people. People like Dr. McKeown and other orthopods and so on and so I had done quite a bit for her medically, but she just used to say, "Well, if you can't accept this, then you can't come. I won't take you next year."

But this went on and on and on and every year she would take us and I never paid a cent for my lodging. I paid for my food and the going rate for the rest of the family.

Each year she got more and more limp and more and more pain and when no one was looking she used a cane for her walks. Every evening she would take a walk through the woods. When the dishes were done and the cabin cleaned up, if she possibly could, and she had her own private little places through the woods. I could show you them all. Her own trails, where she would take ten minutes, or twenty minutes, or half an hour, or even an hour, and maybe go part way up the first Nub for a walk.

I gave her some pills, 292's and anti-arthritic pills, but when she came in to my office in October of 1958 she had lost some weight and that afternoon she was actually sweating with pain. I had mentioned surgery before but she had said no, no; no one was going to operate on her because for sure she would die under the anaesthetic.

"People die from fright, don't they?"

"No, they don't, but you can think they do."

She said that she was so frightened that she would die from fright and that would be that and she didn't want the operation until she couldn't go any longer. That afternoon she came and I can remember arguing with her for at least half an hour that the time had come, that there was nothing more could be done. She had had physio, she had had diothermy and all the other things, and that she would just have to have surgery. So she said, "Would you do it?"

"No."

"Why not? I've got money you know."

"I'm not thinking about money. I don't like to operate on my friends. My real friends. My close friends."

80

In a small voice she said, "Oh, what a compliment."

"You see, we don't operate on our own families."

"But you would do it anyway, wouldn't you?"

"No. Look, believe me, you've got to have the best man in town."

"Aren't you the best man in town?"

"No, Lizzie darling, I'm not the best man. Dr. Sturdy is the best man and I'm going to ask him to see you."

"Oh. I'll go to the coast and see Dr. Preston, he'll do it."

"Alright."

"Are you serious?"

"Dead serious."

So I arranged for her to see Dr. Sturdy and he said yes, she needed a fusion and I could go ahead and do it. He thought I should go ahead and do it anytime. I said, "Don, I want you to do it."

"What?"

"I want you to do it."

"I thought I was a second opinion?"

"You are a second opinion, and I want you to do it."

"What's the matter with you; are you paralysed?"

"No, I don't want to operate on Miss Rummel. I want you do to it."

"You'll help me won't you?"

"Sure, sure, I'll help you, but you got to do it, and you've got to tell her you did it."

"Oh, won't she believe you?"

"No."

So we booked her and she held my hand she said, "The chances I'll die are pretty big, aren't they?"

"The chances that you'll die are not as big as the chances that I'll die overnight. Surgeons die you know."

"The anaesthetic kills so many people."

"The anaesthetic doesn't kill anybody and it's not going to kill you. And when you wake up I'll be holding your hand just like I am now."

So by gosh, we fused her and he. . . . we did it together, but from the actual point of view of surgery he did it. I don't think she ever quite believed me, because she used to say: "He saved my life. He operated on me."

"No, Lizzie darling, Sturdy operated on you."

Well, he actually did do it although I did too. We did it together.

That was January 30, 1959. The operation took about three hours. It was a very difficult one to do because she had a lot of what is called osteoporosis of the acetabulun and a great big cyst that now would give problems to do a total replacement as they now do. And the fusion was done because at that time we were doing what is called osteotomies, which is a much lesser operation but we couldn't do any osteotomy on he because of this huge cyst in the bone, which meant she had tremendous pain.

The other thing which we used to do was to insert, what we call an Austinmoore prosthesis and we couldn't do that because the acetabulun was so damaged. And looking at it in retrospect, I doubt if we could have done what we now call a total replacement, which she subsequently had in the other hip, and it has worked beautifully.

When she got out of the operation we had her in a huge cast, and I went over that night and she was just frantic. She had claustrophobia. The cast ran from her nipples down to the tip of her toe on one side and to her knee on the other. That is pretty total. Its purpose was to keep the hip absolutely still. Because hips don't fuse unless they are kept absolutely still.

So, here she was, and I took her hand and said, "Lizzie, we're both alive."

"Am I alright?"

"Yes, you're alright."

"I can't go another minute. You've got to cut the cast."

"Lizzie, the whole thing depends on this."

"Cut it anyway."

"Alright."

So I went and got the cast cutters and cut the cast and raised it up.

"Thank you."

Now that left her so she was. . . .it wasn't pressing on her belly. After about an hour, I said, "Lizzie, I've got to close it now."

"Alright."

So I closed it and wrapped it up with adhesive. But, she subsequently said, "If you hadn't cut the cast, I would have died in the night, I was so panicky."

She got along fine. I used to go over in the evenings after work and she was on the southwest side of the hospital, and you could see the sunset, but she was still in bed, and you could see the mountains and so I would hold her hand, and she would say, "Alright, what mountains can you see?"

"Oh, I can see Moose Mountain, I can see Cornwall, I can see the Bandit Peak, I can see Mount Rae, and now comes the sunset and the beautiful clouds. It's beautiful Lizzie."

And by golly, she would go to sleep.

This went on and finally we got the cast off and got her up and gave her physiotherapy. In June we got her home. . . .there is a picture of her somewhere. . . . sitting on that porch and she just looked like a ghost.

Dr. J. S. Gardner

*　　*　　*

While in the Calgary General Hospital Lizzie's stay was not all pain, suffering and struggling to maintain equilibrium. Life, as always for Lizzie, was interest in other people and what they were doing. As a magnet draws metal, so Lizzie drew people to her whether she was lying on her back for many months or on her feet at Skoki or Mount Assiniboine.

There would have been a steady stream of people in her hospital room if the door wasn't (theoretically) locked, but in spite of the locked door policy, there still was a steady stream of visitors. Friends and hospital staff came to see her and never forgot her. Years later members of the hospital staff would ask, "How's Miss Rummel?" A current bulletin travelled throughout the hospital, by word of mouth, as to her progress.

When Lizzie was released from hospital five months later, on June 20, 1959, she went to the ranch for two weeks and then back to Jean Waterhouse's home in Banff where she had been living. Jean gave her a bedroom on the main floor of the house so she did not have to climb stairs and tried to get her mobile, taking her out a bit in the car. It was very hard for Lizzie to be so inactive after having lived such an active life. Although she was in a lot of pain when she first came home from hospital, she was always cheerful and welcomed many visitors and entertained them in Jean's garden.

At this time the Waterhouse home was a very active house. While Lizzie entertained her many friends, Jean's three children were also busy with their friends coming and going. Philippe DeLaSalle and Hans Gmoser were some of the frequent callers at the Waterhouse home.

For Lizzie the summer of 1959 meant no Assiniboine. While she was struggling to recover her mobility her long time friends Muriel Gratz and Liana Van Der Bellen ran Sunburst Camp.

Muriel, a school teacher and principal in Banff, is one of those rare individuals, like Lizzie, who loved the mountains and everything about them and could not only meet the challenge of the mountains but the challenge of running Lizzie's camp after an exhausting school year. Liana, also loved the mountains and had the strong constitution with which to meet their challenges as well.

Muriel and Liana's first guest of the season was a young man, Robert Kelly, from Australia, who was walking from Calgary to

Vancouver with one packhorse. This encounter with such an unique individual lent a certain excitement to their summer. Muriel and Liana were thrilled to meet the many interesting and provocative characters who came to Sunburst Camp, either to stay or just to have a cup of tea.

Lizzie slowly recovered from her long hospital stay under the careful eyes of Dr. Gardner, Jean Waterhouse and her many friends. The following spring she approached Dr. Gardner and asked, "Do you think I could get into Assiniboine?"

Gardner, sensing Lizzie's need to be at Sunburst, answered, "Yes, we'll put you on a horse and in you go."

Thus, Smitty Gardner, along with Lizzie's sister Nina and her husband Paddy Rodgers, drove with Ray McBride to the end of Spray Lake and Ray's horse corral. Here Ray had a quiet horse especially picked for Lizzie to ride.

*   *   *

We put the saddle on and we had a great big piece of foam, four or five inches thick, which we put on the saddle, and then we just lifted her up bodily and put her on it. We packed all the packhorses with all the stuff for the camp. Lizzie sat with her good leg at right angles. . . .she really sat on her other hip. We tied her foot in a rope, it was a very quiet horse, and got her to Bryant Creek Warden's cabin. There we lifted her off and she had a cup of tea and a little rest. We packed up the horses again and away we went.

I can see her and Nina going up Bryant Creek as if it was yesterday and I said, "By gosh, they're going to make it; she's going to make it."

Just then there was the biggest hullabaloo that ever happened. One of the packhorses was a real cayuse and Paddy had packed it. There was some tin somewhere and it rattled and made the horse jump and startled it and it went charging off down through the meadow and bucked everything off. Picking up the stuff we found a long parcel broken right in half and in the middle of it was a great big tin of Roger's syrup which had spilled out and got on her guest book, and there was Paddy Rodgers with his handkerchief licking it. He wanted to get it off where it was written on before it would smear. He was licking the pages apart and shaking it and wiping it with his hankerchief, and he said, "Oh, run and get some water quick."

I ran and got water to wash it. Of course, Lizzie and Nina didn't hear any of this until the next day. We told her the next morning when she was looking for the guest book. We had it out drying.

We stayed in a few days and I think I came out alone, and she spoiled me terribly. . . .terribly. I had the best cabin, I had the best blankets, I had the best food, and so on and so forth.

Dr. J. S. Gardner

* * *

Nina and Paddy stayed for about a week to help Lizzie get the camp in order. Later Ruth Wilson, from Canmore, went in and helped her run the camp for the summer.

That summer Lizzie got about with two canes and later with one cane.

* * *

I think I told her I wouldn't allow her to go in unless she did as I said, so she had to use two canes. She got so she could walk further and further with her little trips. We went in later that summer, as a family, and she was doing alright and whoever was helping her was very good.

Dr. J. S. Gardner

* * *

Ken and Vera Hatch from Toronto were among the guest that summer, when they signed Lizzie's guest book they wrote her a little poem.

Have you had a kindness shown?
Pass it on.
It was not given to thee alone.
Pass it on.
Let it travel down the years,
Let it wipe another's tears,
Till in Heaven the deed appears.
Pass it on.

The kindnesses that Lizzie had shown to others came back to bless her when she was struggling to make a go of Sunburst Camp in spite of her handicap. How well she treasured this lovely poem and how well Lizzie's friends treasured her.

Lizzie was back in harness. In spite of her operation and having to use a cane, she managed very well. By the time the following spring came around she was in good spirits and health. She walked into Skoki Lodge on snowshoes, using two ski poles for support, and operated Skoki Lodge from March 7th to April 27th for spring skiing. She was only back home long enough to get organized for another summer camp, purchase staples and head into Sunburst Lake.

During this summer of 1961 Jim Gray, Garnet and Franz Dopf and George McCurdy climbed Mount Assiniboine, on July 8th, taking with them Lizzie's two ice axes. (One may have been her mother's.) A commemorative photograph was taken on the summit of the mountain for Lizzie with her ice axes in full view. It was a great thrill to Lizzie that, at least, her ice axe had climbed Mount Assiniboine, since she could no longer climb and had never climbed her special mountain herself.

As time went on Lizzie continued to endear people to her. She had an ability to draw friends from every walk of life. Her aristocratic upbringing in Germany and her rough ranch life in Canada, enabled her to talk to anyone on any level. She was like two people Ken Jones often said. Drawn from two entirely different cultures she was very adaptable. While on one hand she could be entirely at home with Charlie Hunter, a farmer and packer who did his shirt up with a nail; she could also be perfectly at home with surgeons, botanists and musicians.

Lizzie could talk for hours about the plants and flowers with Arnold Brigden, the amateur botanist and professional lithographer from Winnipeg, and could also talk for hours with Charlie Hunter and Ray McBride about the mountains and trails.

*   *   *

She gave tea to everyone in sight. You would go along there to Sunburst about three o'clock in the afternoon and you would meet everybody. I said to her, "Lizzie, you can't go on serving tea and cookies to everybody."

"I'll do as I please, thank you."

Nobody ever paid for it. A very few people would leave silver. Very occasionally. Poor old Erling. . . .he would say, "Yeah, yeah, and my clients go over there for afternoon tea and we have tea here. Lots of it." So he would go over for tea too.

I saw him one time sitting on a horse drinking a cup of tea. He said, "Lizzie had this tea and it was going to waste."

Her tea always tasted so good when you'd get in there, or back from a hike.

It got so with all of us that we were going to Assiniboine.

"Well, what for?"

"Well, it's beautiful."

"Oh, more beautiful than other places?"

"Well, I guess it's not more beautiful than Jasper and Banff, but then you see, Lizzie's there."

I went because Lizzie was there. I haven't been since.

It's so hard to explain the quality that drew me to her. As I say, I loved her but I don't know how I loved her. I bet a lot of people, if you pushed them, would tell you the same thing. She was so. . . .first of all, she was such a wonderful person. She exuded her own worth as a person. You just watched her doing things and she just exuded a competence in a quiet way. But human too. She could swear if need be but she had a way of relaxing under stress which was fascinating. But then, you hadn't met her for more than five or ten minutes until she knew what your real problem was. You could have a toothache and she could give you the right stuff for it. Or, you had a sprained ankle. . . .she'd wrap it up, or you were hungry and she'd feed you. Or, you needed a cup of tea — she'd give you a cup of tea, or you thought you wouldn't find your way somewhere. She was the most helpful person in that respect but quite beyond that she knew what was bothering you. She wouldn't tell you what to do about it but you could tell her your problems. . . .and this is what counselling is all about.

"She sure made me feel good. I haven't felt this good for weeks."

"Well, what did she tell you?"

"I don't know."

Lizzie had this down to a T (counselling) — down to a fine point. She would give you a cup of tea and in a very few minutes you would be relating to her, in detail, your heartbreak, or whatever it was. She would be helping you through your heartbreak.

If you were camping you would go back for more.

"Where are you going? Are you going down to the lake."

"No, I'm going over to see Miss Rummel."

"For tea?"

"No, no, just passing by."

"Oh, are you going to Cerulean Lake?"

"Well, I guess. I just want to see Lizzie again."

"Oh!"

. . . .or if you are at her place. . . .

"Who was that?"

"Oh some people I know."

"What were they doing?"

"Oh, they just dropped in."

"What's her problem?"

"Well, her brother committed suicide last year and she needs someone to help her."

"Who's helping her?"

"I don't know, but she's going to come again tomorrow."

"Who the hell are you Miss Rummel?"

"I don't know, they just like to come back, that's all. I didn't do anything."

"You must have done something. Didn't you give her a cup of tea?"

"No, it wasn't tea time."

"What did she come in for?"

"She said she wanted to see me again."

Now, if you can analyse this you're wonderful, because nobody else can. That is what her secret was. That is why Neil Brown said, "I don't care where you go, you gotta go and see Miss Rummel, period. You have to meet this lady." That is how the whole thing of our friendship started.

She always said the truth. She was honest and straightforward. She always saw right into the middle of everyone. I have often wondered. . . .I've laid awake wondering. People who can help other people. You know how humans go on.

"Oh, I'm just over breaking my leg."

"Oh, are you really? Oh, you see I broke mine six years ago."

Do you follow. . . .we all do this, everybody does this. Two guys meet. They are talking about their wives, or their stock market thing, or themselves in two minutes.

I think when Lizzie came out here as a competent young teenager, competent in music and art, physical things, she knew the world, she could speak Italian, German, French and English. She had everything. And so you know, in one day she had nothing and they were living in a log house. She was used to laces and doilies and showers and music and fluff and down and servants at the slightest request. She was looking at log walls and I think this hurt. Hurt enough that she knew she was strong enough within herself to help anybody who was hurt. Nobody had any more hurt than she had, except she wasn't afraid to hear anybody's story.

I used to tease her a little bit. . . . "Say, the life you came from. Did you ever want to go back? In your mind?"

"What do you think in about the third or fourth year of the war?"

"Oh."

Can you imagine, milking cows, scrubbing out barns, standing in the cold, looking at logs. This big hurt was such a big hurt that I don't think she ever got over it much.

That is why I say, people like talking about themselves. . . .that's why you say, "I am just over breaking my leg."

"Oh, have you? That's too bad. You see I broke mine six years ago."

You say that to help them.

I don't think she did any of this for self aggrandizement. She did it because she inherently liked to help the other guy because she knew he, or she, suffered something and she was confident that she had seen enough suffering that she could help. She knew the way to suffer, so she could help the other guy. This is what this lady had. The inherent ability to work out the other guy's heartbreak, or problem, or hurdle or whatever. She wouldn't solve it, she would listen and she would help those people, and they would keep coming back for more.

Dr. J. S. Gardner

*   *   *

CHAPTER XIII

A Tragic Accident

AT THIS TIME LIZZIE WAS STILL SPENDING HER WINTERS IN BANFF AND living with Jean Waterhouse in her big house, under the shadow of tall spruce trees. Then Jean married Jim Walls on March 25, 1960, acquiring three step children to add to her own family of three. Lizzie decided to move from Jean's house to make room for the enlarged family.

On the shore of the Bow River, near the boathouse, Lizzie found a small, whitewashed log cabin which had been the Banff Curling Clubhouse. The cabin had long windows from which Lizzie could watch the curling on the Bow River. The cabin had been built in 1898 by Scottish curling enthusiasts. Muriel Gratz said "It was the coldest place on the face of the earth", but Lizzie loved the little cabin. It was cute, Muriel said, especially the way the cold water would have to run all the time or else it would freeze. The cabin now rests in Heritage Park in Calgary and from it can be seen the Ranchers' Hall from Millarville which used to be on Fisher ranch land and in which Lizzie had danced during Millarville festivities.

Although Lizzie didn't have many household furnishings for her new home, she did have nice steer hides on the floor and a gas stove struggled to keep the chill out of the cabin.

From her cabin home in Banff, Lizzie continued to go to Mount Assiniboine each summer and operate Sunburst Camp. One evening at Mount Assiniboine, when it was almost twilight, Lizzie left Sunburst cabin for her habitual evening walk. She followed one of her little trails up the hill towards the first Nub on The Nub Mountain. It was a beautiful little place of which she was very fond. Finding a tree had fallen across the trail she tried pulling it off the trail only to have it break. When it broke, she was thrust backwards on the trail, falling six to nine meters. As she fell her hip broke, the one which had been fused only three years earlier.

As Lizzie lay on the steep slope in great pain, she realized she was not in a safe place so she crawled down to the bottom of the hill to where it levelled off onto a sort of land bench. While she hollered for help, her heart sunk in dispair because she was sure no one could hear her. The spot where she fell was away back in the bush — there was a gully and then a flat marshy place between the hill she was on and the cabin, so no one would probably hear her call.

Lizzie had told the girl who was working for her that summer that she would only be out about twenty or thirty minutes, so when she did not return the guests went out into the dark night and searched for her. Erling Strom was immediately notified Lizzie was missing. He and Dr. Golden, one of his guests, and Ruth Green, a physiotherapist, went over to Sunburst Cabin to help in the search.

It was after midnight when Lizzie was found. Someone built a fire beside her and others brought lots of blankets which they wrapped around her. In the morning a stretcher was brought and Lizzie was carried down to her cabin, placed on the dining table where Dr. Golden and Ruth Green splinted her leg.

In the meantime, Glen Lewis, one of Floyd Smith's men (an outfitter in the area), got on his horse and rode through the dark out Bryant Creek to Spray Lake. At the end of the trail he took his pick-up truck and tore into Canmore over the rough and horrendous road along the west side of Spray Lakes Reservoir, to phone for help. Lewis made the trip via horse and truck in four and one-half hours — record breaking time. A distance of eighteen kilometers by trail and forty-eight kilometers by truck.

In Canmore Lewis quickly found a telephone and phoned Dr. J. S. Gardner at his home, getting him out of bed about five o'clock in the morning. Blurting out the story he asked Gardner if he could get a helicopter to go and get Lizzie.

*   *   *

Well, I didn't know anybody that had a helicopter, but I got the yellow pages out and got the Bullock Brothers — got him out of bed and told him it was a serious situation. I said there was a lady in the mountains with a broken hip and she was in very bad shape, and could they fly her out.

He said, "Oh, we could think about it."

"How much would it cost?"

"I don't know."

"Do you know where Assiniboine is?"

"Good heavens, no. I don't know where Assiniboine is."

Lizzie's cabin on the Bow River as it now stands in Heritage Park, Calgary.

"Have you got a map?"

"No, no, I haven't got a map."

"Well look, I am a practising doctor and I can tell you where it is and I'll bring a map. Where can you meet me?"

"Can I meet you at the Beacon Hotel?"

"I'll meet you there in ten minutes."

"No, make it six o'clock. I can't be there in ten minutes."

"Alright."

So I jumped into my clothes and rushed up to the Beacon Hotel and he brought his brother along.

"Whatever it costs, you gotta go and get this lady."

"Alright."

"I don't know how many miles away it is. I should think it is seventy-five miles, so I don't know how much gas you will need. She is a lady who weighs about one hundred and forty-five to one hundred and fifty pounds and has a broken hip. There are people there who will have her splinted so you can get her into the copter, and then you are to bring her to the General Hospital. While you are there I'll make all the arrangements with the traffic, the police, the whole bit. There is an open field in front of the General Hospital and whatever happens, put her down there."

"Well, we can't put a chopper down in the middle of the city."

"By then I'll have permission."

"You won't get permission."

92

"I'll get permission."

I knew a sergeant in the. . . .

Bulloch said, "You're to come."

"Look, you got to bring her out and it is at seven thousand feet."

"You can't come. I can't lift you and her off and myself and the gas I will need to take in and out."

"That's right."

"No, I'll have to look after her on the way out."

"Tell them to give her a hypo, put her in and then you bring her out, and if she starts getting short of breath, push her chest."

"I've got to fly the chopper."

"Watch her carefully. Have you any oxygen?"

I don't know whether he had oxygen. In any event, I got the chief of police and a sergeant I knew and I told them the story. They said, "Oh yes, when do you think she will be there?"

"Well, around eleven. Between eleven and twelve."

"Well, you got permission, but you don't know where you got it. There are wires you will have to be careful about. Has he got a radio?"

"No, I don't think so, but I told him where they are and to watch out for the telephone poles and wires and so on."

"When we hear the chopper we'll stop the traffic coming both ways so there will be no trouble."

I got the people in the x-ray organized so that as soon as we heard the chopper I would signal them and they would run out into the yard with a stretcher. Eventually, the chopper came and circled the hospital, whereupon every window in front of the hospital had fourteen people looking out, and I had these kids in the x-ray, who all knew me well, and I briefed them as to what was going to happen. They were all eager beavers to do what was right. The chopper came down and they stopped the traffic and we got Lizzie out. Then I said to Bulloch, "Get the hell out of here."

The City hadn't given us permission, so he got out of there right away with his chopper and we wheeled her into the x-ray; x-rayed her and took her right to the operating room. No one, had she been the queen of England, could have been looked after more quickly — because everybody was on my side.

For a long time I was the doctor who had a patient brought into the front yard of the hospital in a helicopter. Dr. McKeown said, "I've seen everything. You get your patients brought in by chopper."

When we looked at the x-rays it was broken right off. Just below the fusion. I was determined that we wouldn't cut her. She had said, "Please don't cut me again."

By golly, I set that thing with brute strength, I don't mind telling you. I put traction on it, and you can wind up the crank and can pull her leg so hard that you pull it apart and then I got under with my shoulder. . . . and my helper, panicking, said, "Look, you'll break it again."

"I don't give a damn."

And I just pushed it up and got it set and put it in another cast and she was almost five months in the cast. In the same kind of a cast. And that got better.

I might as well tell you, I held her hand for lots of hours. She was really upset. I had phone calls here — eight, nine, ten, eleven o'clock at night.

"It's from Miss Rummel, can you come?"

This woman was so upset that I would go. I would go over and just hold her hand. It really was terrible. That is why, for the rest of her life, she would look at me and say, and I used to say, "It's a lie, and you shouldn't say it." . . . . She would look at anyone and say, "He saved my life." And she believed it.

She wasn't as bad as she thought she was psychologically, but she just needed help. You can imagine the bond. I've tried to look back and tried to imagine what kind of a bond it was between us. I said to her many times: "You know Lizzie, I don't think I could fall in love with you enough to be married to you if we were both single."

"Neither could I."

"But yet I love you differently than I love my sisters and closer in lots of ways, and yet I can't think of you as my mother." She was only. . . .nearly nine years older.

We used to laugh about this, but from that day forward she used to say, "I want you to meet Dr. Gardner. He is the man who saved my life twice."

"Lizzie, if you keep saying that, I am going to say the most ridiculous things about you."

"You do anyway."

You can imagine how little I could pay her.

Dr. J. S. Gardner

*   *   *

Once more Lizzie drew people to herself as she lay on her hospital bed for many months.

This tragic accident happened on July 24th, 1962. Lizzie was flown to the Calgary General Hospital on the 25th, the cast came off four and a half months later, on December 10th, but Lizzie was not out of hospital until January 21st, 1963, except for a couple of days over Christmas when she went to the ranch.

From hospital, Lizzie went to Neil Brown's home in Calgary to convalesce until February 12th, at which time she returned to her little cabin along the Bow River in Banff.

February 12, 1963.
Back in my cabin in Banff after an absence of six months.
Thanks to my dear family, Dr. Gardner and all my many friends.

That spring of 1963 Lizzie struggled once more to regain her mobility and become active again. She was very sick and pale and having great difficulty recovering when a visit from Ray Heimbecker cheered her up, giving her the push which she needed to make a full recovery. Ray Heimbecker was the young boy whom Lizzie had told, in 1938 at Erling Strom's lodge at Mount Assiniboine, that he could become a surgeon because he peeled potatoes so beautifully.

*   *   *

Ray Heimbecker had gone to the University of Toronto and someone there interested him in research and, fortunately, it was in blood research.

Lizzie and Ray Heimbecker at Assiniboine. 1967.

At that time one of the biggest problems was blood clotting after operations. If the clot goes to your brain or your heart you die. You can get a clot in your leg or in your abdomen, or even in your arm, but mostly in your lower abdomen or in your leg and the clot goes to your heart and you die. What researchers were trying to find out was: what starts this clotting?

Heimbecker went to either Chicago or Cleveland and got a scholarship to go into this research. At that time I was terribly interested in post-operative thrombosis and pulmonary emboli that kill people. You could have the healthiest person in the world, take their appendix out and in a few days they were dead. The whole western world was interested in how this started.

There is a thing in the blood called Rouleau Formation, and that is when the red blood cells pile up on each other like little donuts. Prior to clotting the blood will form rouleaus, and the idea was to try and find out what initiated this rouleau formation and how did it happen. That was what Heimbecker's research was all about. Heimbecker worked out a whole method of research that initiated the research into how a clot actually formed. He got into the medical press and became famous. And I heard about him and I heard that he was an Alberta boy. I had friends in Toronto, professors and so on, so I said, "When is Heimbecker coming back?"

One of my big moments in my surgical career of that time was to meet and shake hands with Ray Heimbecker — this fabulous person.

A friend of mine who set up the cardiovascular unit at the Toronto General Hospital was just as interested, so when Heimbecker came back to Canada he grabbed him.

"You're going to work with me."

That was Dr. Bill Bigelow who was then the professor of cardiovascular surgery. So he went and worked with Bill Bigelow and did heart surgery and it was just when open heart surgery was starting — pacemakers, not by-passes yet, blue baby operations, the whole thing opened up in about three or four years in the early sixties, late fifty-nine. Bigelow was the man who started hypothermia; where you put people in a bathtub of ice, cool them right down and then operate on them — you can open the heart for ten or fifteen minutes and they won't die. The brain doesn't get destroyed. Bill Bigelow set that thing going and he is known throughout the world because of his hypothermia studies. He worked it out with woodchucks.

Heimbecker got in on this and then he became his associate. He did various things. One thing that put him on the surgical map in the English speaking world, maybe the whole world, was. . . .You see if you have a heart attack a piece of the heart muscle goes dead because the blood supply has stopped and so theoretically, if you could go in just as the heart attack happened and you could delineate where it had happened and then burst (people die three or four days after the heart attack) and sew that up, you save their lives.

Ray took a dozen or more cattle and gave them heart attacks of that nature and then went in and sewed up the place and some of them survived. And then he did a case — a fifty-six year old man had a heart attack — the blood had clotted in the hospital, within an hour he was in there and he could electrically delineate where the heart attack affected the muscle and the man survived. Unfortunately, about a month later he died of pneumonia.

Every year at the Canadian Royal College of Surgeons there is what's called the surgical lecture and if you give the surgical lecture at the Royal College you are on top of the pile. That year, at the Royal College Dr. Ray Heimbecker was the speaker and he talked about this procedure and the place was packed — there wasn't even standing room — and there was a standing ovation for Heimbecker. There had never been a standing ovation before. The first person to stand up was the professor of pathology at the University of Toronto who was world renowned for his work in pathology and had written six or seven books in pathology.

I went up to Ray and he said, "Gee, what are they standing up for?"

"I don't know what the others are standing up for but did you see Bill Boyd stand up?"

"Bill Boyd didn't stand up, did he?"

"He was the first man up applauding."

All of this that would happened to Ray I would bring to Lizzie. Once or twice she said, "You're lying aren't you?"

"No, I'm not lying. I am telling you the truth. He is one of the big shots in Canada and he is known all across the States."

After that second hip operation, when Lizzie was very sick and struggling to live in that drafty cabin in Banff, Ray Heimbecker came to give the surgical lecture at the Canadian Medical Association convention in Banff. I was the logistics person who set up the convention. One day Ray came sailing along and we got him put up and so on and he asked me, "What about Lizzie?"

"She's in her cabin. She is not very well, she looks pale, but she is better than she looks and she would love to see you."

"Well, I only have this one afternoon that I can manage. Do you think if it doesn't rain I could take her for a canoe ride up to the Vermillion Lake?"

"I don't think, I know. Can you lift her?"

"Sure."

"Get a big canoe and lift her in it and wrap her all up right and paddle her up the river."

"What'll I take to eat?"

"Anything you like, but she likes ice cream."

So by golly, he gave his lecture and then he just got out of there, hell bent for leather. He bought a box with two bricks of ice cream in it for two people. He had enough food for six people and he took her up there along the Bow River to Vermillion Lake. That was one of the biggest afternoons in either one of their lives. He will talk about it for the rest of his life.

Dr. J. S. Gardner

*   *   *

CHAPTER XIV

Charlie Hunter and Other Stories

LATE IN JUNE OF 1963 LIZZIE RETURNED TO SUNBURST LAKE AND HER cabin. Smitty Gardner, her sister Nina and her nephew's wife, Pat, went with her and helped her set up the camp.

> Well! Lizzie! Here we are!! — as planned — A wonderful experience for me to see you back again in this Haven — which only proves that all things are possible — nearly. Thanks for a wonderful holiday.
>
> *Smitty*
> *Sunburst guest book.*

This was one of the summers when Mehitabel, the tame female moose, frequently came around Lizzie's cabin. Normally the moose hung around Erling Strom's lodge but when the pickings were poor there she would amble over to Lizzie's place and try to grab the bread which Lizzie hung in a sack under the porch roof. The sack had a bell attached to it so when the moose tried to get it the bell rang. Lizzie would get up out of bed and bombard the moose with pieces of firewood. In the morning she would have to retrieve the firewood from all over the front lawn. Mehitabel lived in the area for many years and when she had a calf she brought it with her and taught it how to beg for food as well.

Moose were not the only animals which could be seen near Lizzie's cabin. One day a guest of Lizzie's, Samuel Frothingham from Princeton, New Jersey, saw a cougar. He had been fishing in Cerulean Lake. . . .

> . . . .he was burning up some lunch papers when the cougar first loped by only sixty feet away. After some more

fishing and picture taking he sat down, waiting for his wife to show up. Suddenly the cougar appeared a second time, and was now coming towards him. Frothingham had the presence of mind and coolness of spirit to photograph the cougar, a very rare and privileged sight.

Erling Strom

That September John Forli, of Banff, built the foundation for a new cabin behind Lizzie's cookhouse cabin and put a new floor on the existing cabin, built two new toilets, a stone wall and did some landscaping for Lizzie. The next year Charlie Hunter and Lizzie's sister Jane built the new cabin.

Also, Hans Gmoser came into Sunburst with Christa Weller and they climbed Sunburst Face on September 28th, the fifth ascent, in a mere three hours. Lizzie silently cheered from the shore of Sunburst Lake and kept the tea kettle hot.

Every year many friends of Lizzie's were climbing mountains in the area. Of course, the most popular mountain was Assiniboine but other noble peaks were also ascended and many cups of tea at "Lizzie's Place" refreshed them on their return, while they recounted the climb.

Lizzie's cabin, and in fact her home wherever she was — Skoki, Sunburst, Banff — was always a place for tea and conversation. Many a philosophical turn of mind was well discussed, and many a valuable tidbit of mountain information changed hands over a cup of tea in Lizzie's presence. Broken hearts found sympathy and love across the kitchen table ladened with tea, cookies and kindness. Surely Lizzie knew the value of a therapeutic cup of tea.

In the Canadian Rocky Mountains it is a tradition when there is no solution to a problem, or the burdens of the day are just too much to handle, "Let's have a cuppa tea" somehow changes the look of even the worst problems. Mary Conway exemplified this when she wrote in the Alpine Club of Canada Journal in 1948:

A tea tent is certainly a morale booster in any camp and I can only weep for my lost youth in the States where I was unaware that such refinements existed. Aside from its merits as a beverage, tea has a unique psychological value. How many parties would have been stranded high in the mountain vastness had not the prospect of tea called forth superhuman feats of effort and skill! How many little tidbits of gossip would have died an undernourished death had not the tea tent provided an audience. If I learned nothing else from my stay in Canada, I am forever grateful that I learned to appreciate that nectar of the mountain gods, hot tea.

As usual, Lizzie's cups of tea were still available to mountain travellers and Lizzie still enjoyed their company. She did so well during the summer that she stayed at Sunburst Lake until well into October and enjoyed every minute.

Every summer, for many years, Charlie Hunter went to Mount Assiniboine and helped Lizzie and Erling Strom, lending his own special flavor to their camps. Charlie was a man of great devotion to the people he loved. A bachelor all his life, he left the packer's life in Banff and returned to his parents' ranch near Pincher Creek, Alberta, when they were too old to ranch and operated the ranch until their deaths. When well past retirement age he helped Lizzie and Erling Strom for no pay. He did it because he loved them.

*   *   *

One time I wanted to go there alone and I wanted to sleep on the promotory above Lizzie's cabin. Lizzie said they would put the blue tent up there, but they never got the tent up so the last year she was there I took up a big tent as the blue one was being used. I put it up but the poles were a little short. I tied it up anyhow, but didn't put all the stakes in. I then went down to supper in the cabin. After supper I went up and there was Charlie taking it all down. He had gotten longer poles and put in all the stakes. I kept saying, "Charlie look, this can go there and this there."

So he looked at me very firmly and said, in his slow drawl, without so much as a smile, "I put up the tent for Miss Rummel."

I crept quietly away.

Charlie was a wonderful fisherman and Lizzie got so she hated frying fish. She got him trained so he wouldn't fish as much. He knew where to go to fish.

One day he broke his fishing reel, so he fixed it. It broke again, so he fixed it again. He had to send for a new one but in the meantime he told someone to get him a new one in Banff but not to pay a big price. Just to make do until he got the good one. They got him one made in Japan and he caught fish and it broke, he caught fish and it broke. He kept fixing it and fixing it and fixing it, but finally the new one came, the good one. He took the Japanese reel which kept breaking and put it on the centre of the chopping block, and got the eight pound sledge hammer with a long handle on it (Lizzie was watching from the shadow of the cabin.) and started pounding the reel: "Those Goddamn sons-of-bitches."

Wham, wham, wham. . . .and he hit that thing until it was as thin as tissue paper, cursing all the time at those "sons-of-bitches" at the top of his lungs — he just screams. It had broken so much and so often.

One time I said to Lizzie, "You know, there is all that pile of wood up behind the cabin. I could split that and it wouldn't interfere with Charlie at all."

"Yes, I know, but I don't know what he would think of it and we mustn't upset him. He just gets so upset."

"Well, there is that other axe there. He doesn't use that axe and that wood up there, he won't split that."

"Well, I don't know whether we should."

"Oh, the hell with it, I don't know where he is. I'll go and chop some." I had to chop some wood.

"Yeah, but if you see him coming just come in and pretend you're having coffee or tea."

"Alright."

By gosh, I was chopping away and there I saw him coming around the cabin and right away he looked up and saw me. There was no use pretending then, he actually saw me with the axe in my hand and the whole bit. He went over to his chopping block that was lower down and closer to the lake and he looked all around to see if anybody. . . .I think I had chopped a little down there and Lizzie stopped me. . . .and he walked up and he sat on the edge of the pile of logs and I kept chopping away. I didn't know what the hell to say, and the best thing to say is nothing, so then I got stopped and I picked up another block.

"Hello Charlie." You have to yell at him as he can hardly hear.

"Hello."

I thought, well here it comes, I might as well brace my feet.

"I see you've had an axe in your hand before."

"Yeah, a little bit."

He just got off the pile of logs and walked away. That's all he said.

Lizzie said, "You silly, why did you wait so long?"

"You said he wouldn't be back until five or so. I didn't have a chance. He came around the corner and there he was looking right at me."

When I told her what he said she nearly fell over laughing.

"Didn't he say anything else?"

"No."

"He must like you."

"He's got no reason to like me."

"Well, I was sure scared. I was just scared of what he would say."

Dr. J. S. Gardner

*   *   *

The first time I saw him at Lizzie's I saw him splitting wood and I can always tell when a man knows what he is doing. I said to him, "It looks like that's not the first time you used an axe?"

He started telling me how he was raised on a bush farm in British Columbia. He told me he was hitting logs at twelve years old.

He knew how to handle an axe.

Charlie Hunter

*   *   *

One time one of our dearest friends went up there and I told Lizzie he was an avid fisherman. Charlie took to this school teacher who is still teaching school, who stutters, and Charlie got to like this boy. This boy had a little hesitation in his speech and not many friends and Charlie liked him. He took him to his best fishing hole and came back with fifty-seven fish. Don would still be fishing there but Charlie told him they had caught enough.

I said to him, "Who is going to clean all these?"

"Well, I guess we'll have to."

So we dumped them all out and divided them into three and I started cleaning and Don started cleaning and Charlie was up talking to Lizzie. He came down and looked at us and he cleaned his in half the time.

Boom, boom, boom. And then he came over and just pushed me right away from the fish.

"I clean my own fish."

"Charlie, I could clean a few."

He just pushed me right away and Lizzie was watching. I just thought she would die laughing.

I don't know how long Charlie worked for Lizzie. He was there every year that we were there and we first went in 1956. Fifteen or sixteen years probably. He was a guide with horses. The first few years we went he had horses and camped away off in the bush and didn't stay at her place at all. Nobody knew where his camp was. He had it in a different place every year so nobody knew, except maybe Erling knew. He worked for Erling too.

One time he came with his packhorse and his saddle horse and he had a fish that long hanging from the saddle. I rushed up to him and said, "Oh, Charlie, where did you get that fish?"

"I've forgotten."

"Did you catch it?"

"Well, nobody else did."

"Gee, I didn't know there were fish that big here."

"Well, if you'd been around here as long as I have been you would know where there were fish of all sizes. I wanted a big one. I'm going to cook this and put it in a can so it will keep. It'll last me three or four days."

"Where did you get it?"

"Well, I've forgotten. I don't remember very well."

Lizzie told me he had only been gone a short time.

Two or three years later I was down below Cerulean Lake and there is a winding stream with overhanging branches and moss and so on and I was going along and there was a tremendous rush in the water and I looked and there were a couple of fish this long and one this long. What Charlie had done was go down there and pick it out with his bare hands. They were in little holes and I could have caught one. There was a moose wallow down below it and a lot of people would go down to the moose wallow and look for moose.

You weren't supposed to fish in Elizabeth Lake. I would say, "Yes, but Lizzie, there are some big fish in there and some dandy trout in there."

"You really want to go fishing?"

"Yes, but I want to go down to Wedgewood, because I always could catch fish down there."

"Why don't you try Elizabeth Lake? It will be early, nobody will be around."

"Well, what if I caught some?"

"Well."

"I hate to do that."

"Go ahead. If anybody deserves to have fish out of Elizabeth Lake you do."

So I went over and I caught three fish. I hid them in the bush and put moss and water around them and went down and caught ten at Wedgewood. I came back and it was a hot afternoon and I think they were serving supper. Lizzie came out and said, "Oh, we wondered where you were. It's late, and we're having supper."

"I'm sorry I'm late but it is a long walk back."

"I hope you didn't get any fish."

"Yes, I did. What's the limit? I haven't got the license yet."

"I'll sell it to you in the morning."

"Sell it to me tonight."

"No, no, no. You haven't got any money."

"What's the limit?"

"You know what the limit is."

"No, I really, honestly don't."

"Neither do I. How many did you get?"

"Ten's the limit, isn't it?"

"You know full well it's ten."

"Well, damn it, nobody's told me and you haven't even sold me the license yet. I'm in here a week."

"How many have you got?"

"I don't know. I got quite a few down there and the three I got in Elizabeth Lake."

"Did you get three in Elizabeth Lake?"

"Yes."

"Show me them first."

Dr. J. S. Gardner

*   *   *

Elizabeth Lake, situated up a steep slope from Sunburst Lake and nestled against The Nub Mountain, had been named on March 3, 1960, by the Province of British Columbia, through the efforts of a Calgary group of ten people, making "my lake" really Elizabeth's.

CHAPTER XV

Two New Homes

WHILE LIZZIE WAS TOURING EUROPE AND THEN RUNNING SUNBURST Camp at Mount Assiniboine, her mother was living in Banff where she had moved in June 1949. Omi, as Elsa Basilici was called from the time she acquired grandchildren, had moved from the Fisher ranch to Banff to take an oral French course at the Banff School of Fine Arts. Although her three daughters thought this was very humorous (Elsa was already fluent in French) Omi enjoyed the course and, of course, passed with honors.

When Omi first went to Banff she stayed in the residence of the Mineral Springs Hospital, later she moved into a small one roomed cabin behind Jean (Waterhouse) Walls' home. She lived in this cabin in the winter months and moved into another small cabin on the Bow River during the summer. The winter cabin was rented to tourists in the summer. Twice a year she moved, but she always considered her home to be the ranch at Millarville.

Lizzie was overjoyed to have her mother living close to her, as Elsa was now too frail to make the long trip to Mount Assiniboine. Omi had made several trips to Skoki Lodge when Lizzie was there but, then, she was much younger. Having her mother in Banff was a real treat for Lizzie.

Omi's rich, aristocratic background made her a natural ally of Margaret Greenham and Mrs. W. S. Painter, with whom she regularly had Thursday afternoon teas. The three ladies had all been pioneers in the Canadian west and were very active in cultural activities.

While Omi was in Banff she became involved in the small, but growing, library on a volunteer basis. She was an extremely well read person and was always very interested in a wide variety of books, an attribute which she passed on to her daughter Elizabeth.

*   *   *

I met Lizzie's mother before I met Lizzie — in June 1953: a stunningly <u>present</u> and warm lady — and I met her in the presence of Erling Strom in her cabin by the river, beneath the Banff Fine Arts buildings. A "grande dame" — so calm, rich in volumes, folded like velvet into her age and diminished health. Fresh flowers and the 1953 edition of Kazantzakis' "Zorba the Greek" on her reading table next to her arm chair.

Fr. Peter DuBrul

*   *   *

By 1964 Omi's health had severely deteriorated so she could no longer live alone in her small cabin. She chose the independence of living in a senior citizen's home — Medicine Tree Manor in High River. Later she moved to Southwood Nursing Home in Calgary where she died at the age of eighty-eight, on May 7th, 1966.

Elsa von Rummel-Weinmann-Basilici, nee Hirth, had lived in the world shaped by the Hapsburgs and moved into the new world as a pioneer. In a raw and hard country her life changed from luxury to simple living. She never complained but adapted to her circumstances and used her rich cultural background to enrich her own and others' lives. Everyone who came into contact with her enjoyed her wonderful, captivating personality. Elsa's parting was strongly felt by her three daughters and she was deeply missed.

While Lizzie's summers were spent at Mount Assiniboine, she still spent her winters in Banff in the whitewashed log cabin beside the Bow River and visited her mother frequently. Four years after moving into the log cabin, however, the landlord informed Lizzie she would have to move out. In exasperation she complained to Muriel Gratz: "But I'll just be out on the street!"

Since Muriel and Lizzie had previously purchased an apartment building in Banff, Muriel firmly said, "Listen Elizabeth, we have this apartment, you could always live there."

"Do you think I would live in one of those apartments?" Lizzie spluttered.

"It's a lot warmer than where you are living."

An apartment was not Lizzie's kind of living. The apartment was just an investment; the kind of living Lizzie wanted had a hominess to it that the rustic log cabin, with its cowhide rugs provided, but an apartment never could. The cabin, of course, was very picturesque. It was once featured on one of the Reader's Digest magazine covers. Today it reposes in Heritage Park in Calgary, Alberta.

Lovely or not, Lizzie had to move. Rather than live in "one of those apartments" she went house hunting in Canmore with Jean Walls.

Many years earlier, in 1947, Elsa Basilici had legally turned over the nine quarter sections of ranchland which she had purchased, to her three daughters. Each girl received three quarter sections. Jane and Nina, together with their families, farmed and ranched Lizzie's three quarter sections as well as their own. When Lizzie decided to buy a house she sold one of these quarter sections to provide money for the purchase.

In Canmore, a small town situated nineteen kilometers east of the Town of Banff, Lizzie found a small house beside a creek, amongst large evergreen trees, which looked out onto Grotto Mountain. The house was located on the edge of the town and was not quite as rustic as the cabin in Banff, but it did have a casual, comfortable atmosphere which suited Lizzie. The house had been built by Jack Block, formerly of Holland, and its architecture held a European flavor. Lizzie retained the old furniture in the house and moved her books and few possessions into it and it soon acquired an atmosphere and look which was at once unique and distinctive and showed Lizzie's personality in a remarkable way.

CHAPTER XVI

Tales From Assiniboine Days

A LOT OF LITTLE THINGS HAPPENED TO LIZZIE BOTH IN BANFF AND AT Mount Assiniboine, which made her life interesting and unexpected.

One day in 1965 she received a letter from her Tante Johanna in Garmisch, Germany. As she opened the letter a newsclipping fell out. The news story told of a German gentleman who had been holidaying in the Canadian Rockies. A national parks warden had taken this gentleman to a cabin along the Bow River and told him that the Baroness Elizabeth von Rummel lived in it. The gentleman was completely thunderstruck that "the daughter of the unforgetable Gustav Waldau" lived in this humble setting. One can imagine the smile on Lizzie's face as she read the article.

While a German newspaper carried a remark about Lizzie's humble abode on the Bow River, people from Japan came to her other humble abode — the one in Mount Assiniboine Provincial Park.

Five members of the Osaka Alpine Club were guests at Sunburst Camp in the summer of 1966. The Japanese gentlemen had heard about Mount Assiniboine Provincial Park through an American outdoors magazine. They had written to the governments of Alberta, British Columbia and Canada to find out where the park was situated. The government offices in British Columbia (in which province the park is situated) said they had never heard of the park. In spite of the ignorance of the government offices, these five ingenious young men found the park, how to get to it and found Lizzie's camp where they stayed.

Lizzie thoroughly enjoyed the five climbers and the men thoroughly enjoyed Lizzie. Upon their return to Japan, they sent her a gift of a beautiful scarf. A note accompanied the gift which was signed by each individual climber. Beside each name on the note Lizzie wrote her usual identifying remarks to enable her to remember each man.

109

Leader Magog
young man Assiniboine
Magog
stocky one
Assiniboine polite one (tall)

Writing small comments beside people's names was a way in which Lizzie remembered the individual. Often these comments were amusing, but descriptive. e.g. "good looking fat one."

Lizzie always enjoyed meeting climbers from around the world and different parts of Canada. Lloyd Gallagher, a local guide, once brought two, tall young men into the Assiniboine area to mountain climb. Dieter, Victor and Lloyd walked into the area from Spray Lakes. By the time the long hike brought them to Lizzie's camp they were extremely tired. Dieter and Victor were not used to hiking and this was really more than they could comfortably handle. Lizzie gave the men tea and soup and within half an hour the two fellows were snoring furiously. They woke up two or three hours later very embarrassed. They had only meant to drop in for tea. They did, however, end up staying with Lizzie overnight.

The following day the weather was very overcast, but Gallagher attempted to climb Sunburst Peak with the two fellows. Victor and Dieter were not very serious climbers and they spent a lot of time on the mountain yelling, screaming and yodelling. Lizzie could hear them from her cabin and enjoyed knowing they were having a good time. Although the climbers were not going anywhere in terms of vertical progress, they were the type of climbers who couldn't care less about accomplishing a great feat. A good time was more important to them.

Gallagher had known Lizzie for a long time, having met her when he was working for Hans Gmoser at Bugaboo Lodge in the British Columbia mountains. This was, however, the first time he had stayed at Lizzie's camp. He, Victor and Dieter found their stay to be a real treat as there were no other guests (it was late in the season) and it was a good chance to get to know Lizzie.

On the third day of the trip the men tried to climb Mount Assiniboine but got rained out. The three days turned out to be very important to these two men, however, as Lizzie had made a very deep impression upon them. Later, when they would write to Gallagher they would talk about Lizzie, the trip and the wonderful conversations they enjoyed in the evenings in her cabin. Since that time Gallagher has taken Dieter and Victor to Mount Columbia and other big peaks, but they just talk about the days they spent with Lizzie. Lizzie's love of the mountains and her personality were written indelibly on the men's minds.

Many of Lizzie's guests were highly individualistic and many were leaders in their profession. Arnold Brigden, the amateur botanist and professional lithographer from Winnipeg, Manitoba, was a distinctive, marvelous character. He and his wife had been guests of Lizzie's when she managed Skoki Lodge and Brigden also came to Sunburst Camp. Frequently he would hire an outfitter to take him to a spot in the mountains where he could camp and collect wild flowers for his rock garden in Winnipeg.

Brigden negotiated, through Lizzie, in 1966, to secure a guide and horses for a camp on Marvel Pass, south of Mount Assiniboine Provincial Park. He wanted to spend his time collecting plants and was distressingly concerned his guide would be bored if he had to stay at the camp. "He will never have so little to do in his life again," Brigden wrote in one of his many colorful letters to Lizzie. Brigden was an old man at this time and not particularly well, so he eventually had to change his plans and camp at Wonder Pass, which was not far from Mount Assiniboine Lodge. He became ill during his camp stay and was flown out to hospital in Banff. Prior to his illness, and after several weeks at this Wonder Pass camp, Brigden went to Sunburst Lake to visit with Lizzie. He had not, however, had a bath for the duration of his stay, nor had he changed his clothes.

Lizzie and Myrna Collins, took one look at Brigden and popped him into one of the tent-frame cabins, made him strip all his clothes off, which they proceeded to wash. The clothes were in such a terrible condition they had to boil and scrub to get them clean. Forever after Brigden referred to Lizzie's camp as "Sunburst Steam Laundry" and to his Wonder Pass camp as "Gusty Camp."

When Brigden returned to Winnipeg and his wife, Florence, he wrote to Lizzie.

> Have not started a steam laundry here yet — altho Florence suggested — I go to bed for a couple of days — and get all my clothes washed. But no one here — takes my pants off — or — hides my underwear —

The following Christmas Brigden's Christmas card to Lizzie depicted his remembrances of the incident.

Best wishes to the Whole Staff of Sunburst Steam Laundry A.O.B.

Brigden also had the idiosyncrasy of insisting on soft boiled eggs for breakfast. When he was writing to Lizzie in his efforts to secure a guide, one of the requirements was the guide must be able to soft boil eggs. Cooking a soft boiled egg high in the mountains is not as easy as one may imagine. The traditional three minute egg takes much longer to cook the higher the elevation. At 2,165 meters (Sunburst Camp), it

111

takes at least ten minutes to produce a soft boiled egg. The number of minutes required for another elevation will vary.

Brigden's penchant for soft boiled eggs also showed up in Lizzie's guest book.

Henry the Eighth from Gusty Camp
Soft boiled eggs please.

Arnold Brigden was just one of the many delightful characters who came into Lizzie's life.

*   *   *

I was near one of the cabins and happened to look in a certain direction and there was a grizzly so close I could see the wind ruffle its fur. I hustled calmly to the main cabin, alerted Elizabeth and the two of us set up a tremendous clatter with all the pots and pans we could find. We watched the grizzly from the window. It seemed to look at us with a quizzical expression, took its own time and finally ambled off. Remembering where it had been, I later measured the distance from where I had been standing. It was exactly twenty-two feet.

Muriel Gratz

*   *   *

One morning Ken Jones was wandering around, about the last year Lizzie was there, and up washed, on the shore of Sunburst Lake, a big fish — dead. Out a little ways in the lake was another fish, nearly dead. Jones went out and bashed it over the head. Lizzie was heartbroken. They had died in Sunburst Lake. What was ailing them? We would have to get somebody to see what was the matter with the fish. They had died in her precious Sunburst Lake.

So I said, "Everybody dies when they get old. These damn fish were old. They were obviously great big fish and they just died."

"You don't believe that. Something killed them. Somebody has poisoned them."

"Well, what if they are?"

"There are only about a dozen fish in there and I don't want them to be killed."

In the woods, on a steep bank up from the lake, there was a deep hole ten or fifteen feet deep in silt clay, where Lizzie dumped the wash water. In years gone by it was soap that was used to wash dishes and linens, but in the last few years it was detergent.

Detergent is detergent because of the low specific gravity of it. The first detergent that came on the market, medically, was called "137," because it was one hundred and thirty-seven times better as a penetrator than water. All detergents seep through ground or anything faster than water. I don't know how they stack up against gasoline but I think faster than gasoline.

Poor Lizzie didn't know and nobody would tell her, I hope, that she was poisoning the lake herself. (After a wind storm, down at the end of the lake, you could see froth on the water.) I never told her. She never knew. I am sure she didn't know. She would have been heartbroken if she knew she was doing it. That detergent is what happened to her fish. I was positive about that. She was talking about giving up Sunburst then. The wash water should have been dumped up on the hill and it would then take longer to filter through. You can filter water with chloride in it one hundred yards in gravel and it will be pure. The further it filters, the purer it gets, so her wash water should have been carried up the hill and not towards the lake. She didn't know that, nor did anybody else. I think I told Ken Jones one time and he said, "Don't tell her." It would have broken her heart. It may have only killed the fish in that immediate neighbourhood so I am sure there will still be fish in Sunburst.

Dr. J. S. Gardner

*   *   *

There are a lot of little stories in Lizzie's life which make up the whole.

One story concerns Sydney Vallance, a respected mountaineer and Calgary lawyer. He was one of Lizzie's close friends from the very early nineteen forties, or possibly the late nineteen thirties. Lizzie had a birthday party for Vallance at her Sunburst Camp on November 8, 1969. Vallance's daughter Jean Gill and his long time friend Jim Tarrant, of the Alpine Club of Canada, were at the party. The Mount Assiniboine area also held many precious memories for Sydney Vallance and he was deeply touched by Lizzie's kindness in giving him a birthday party in that setting.

About this same time Lizzie had an exciting helicopter ride to the top of Mount Strom (named after Erling Strom), where she was able to get out of the plane and walk around. Seeing the mountains from that elevation was very exciting; especially being so close to Mount Assiniboine itself.

Lizzie was always fortunate, due to her ability to make deep and close friendships, to be given little trips and taken to places which were meaningful to her, but which her arthritis and her age prevented her from seeing under her own steam. For her friends, to see her appreciation was compensation enough for their efforts.

Lizzie was always doing helpful things for other people as well. The year she was sixty-nine years old she helped Siri Strom Davies and Al Johnston run spring skiing camps at Mount Assiniboine Lodge. Jim

Davies flew the guests into the lodge by helicopter and Hans Gmoser, now well into his mountain guiding business, booked two of the weeks the lodge was open for his ski parties. Lizzie always enjoyed going to Mount Assiniboine during the winter months. It all looked so different with several meters of snow on the ground.

Two years after this incident Lizzie was back at Mount Assiniboine Lodge as hostess and cook for Gmoser when he brought in a small skiing party of five. A lot of snow fell at this time and the ski party was delayed a day at Police Meadows, further north, due to poor visibility. Lizzie kept busy tramping out a landing place for the helicopter.

When Gmoser's party left the area three young men showed up on "real cross-country skis, with soft boots and long poles." Two of the fellows remembered Lizzie from Sunburst Camp when she had offered them a tent in a bad storm. Lizzie discovered the fellows were "pretty well all in" when they arrived, so she gave them hot chocolate before they skied over to the Naiset Cabins nearby. To see "real skiers" reminded Lizzie of the type of skiing which used to be done during her days at Skoki Lodge.

While most of Lizzie's time was spent tramping out a landing pad for the helicopter on this occasion, she did not mind this activity. Just being in the Assiniboine area was a real joy and brightened up the long winters when she was not at her beloved Assiniboine.

Backcountry lodges and huts in the Canadian Rocky Mountains always have a guest book in which people sign their names and more often than not, write interesting comments. Lizzie had kept a guest book at Skoki Lodge and she also kept one at Sunburst Lake Camp.

The comments left in Lizzie's guest book give a wonderful insight into Lizzie's personality, the personality of the individual guests and a glimpse of life in the mountains.

Many thanks Lizzie for the happiest summer I have known! Adieu, with best wishes for your continued good health and happiness.

Myrna Collins

Dear Lizzie —
To see the mountain at last.

Maryalice Stewart
Joan Vroom

More fabulous each of twenty-six years — wolverine?
Ray & Anita & Kathleen Heimbecker

Looking for Cambrian echinoderms at Naiset Point above

Gog Lake — found them and got all this beautiful scenery as a bonus!

Jim Sprinkle
Harvard University

It's good to come where Alvin had so many good times.

Marlis Lindsay & Keith Gaetz

I was last here in 1920. The mountains are still the same but the glaciers are smaller. One of the most beautiful areas I have ever known and Miss Rummel one of the kindest ladies.

Phyllis M. Betz (1968)

Too much bickering among the staff! Had to leave — a lazy bunch here. Will bring a new dish dryer next year.

Margaret Gmoser

Many thanks for a marvelous and typical week: sunshine and snowstorms; lost horses (and hikers), helicopters popping in and out; fish jumping on the lakes; the pack rat jumping on the porch; wonderful company and food (even though the chef had departed). Merci!

Liana Van Der Bellen, Montreal

Ninth time in the valley, seven with Lizzie. Once on a pack trip with Ray, once just to the top of Assiniboine Pass when Lizzie was snowbound at Ray's camp — seems I like the place!!! First climb this year up "Smitty's Route" on Sunburst with himself as guide!!!

Gerry Fish, Calgary (1965)

An abundance of wonderful scenery, friendliness (flies)! fish, <u>fun</u>, food and females! Many, many thanks <u>again</u> Elizabeth for a delightful holiday for us all. Next year the sign will be bigger and better and automatic!

Laura, Mary Ann & Smitty Gardner

Sunburst Lake Camp — the experience for a lifetime.
— the best scenery in the mountains
— the friendliest people in the country
— the best hostess anywhere.

Joe Richards, Michigan

Thank you Lizzie for a wonderful vacation — it is good to be back to my first home in the mountains!

Fran Drummond

I wouldn't want to exchange the snowdrifts, porcupines, mosquitos, dishes for anything. I not only became closer to the mountains but closer to nature herself. I am grateful to you Lizzie for having let me share this last month.

Myrna Collins

Worn out from chasing Betts, but happy.

Keir MacGougan
(with Ken Betts)

To a Sunburst Mosquito
(With apologies to Lizzie and Wordsworth)
Ah, sweet Mosquito, do not take thy flight,
A little longer stay in sight.
Here rest your wings when they are weary,
Here lodge as in a sanctuary.
Come often here and fear no wrong
And hearten all with your sweet song. . . .
Yet, sweet Mosquito, be so kind
When I depart tomorrow —
Please do not follow me about
But feed on those who stay behind. . . .

Liana Van Der Bellen

Ray and I have tried very hard to make this period without you as successful for you as possible. I sincerely hope we have won. Your absence has been deeply felt.

Ruth Wilson
(Lizzie in hospital with a broken hip.)

Walked from Canyon Dam — 19 miles.

Jane Fisher (58 yrs.)
Nina Rodgers (56 yrs.)

Will be back to get even with the inhabitants of Cerulean.

Muriel Gratz

Words are inadequate.

Jean Waterhouse

Enroute to Paris. It's a hard choice!

Joe Plaskett

Grateful for having had the privilege of meeting you and your kind and charming hospitality. The hours we were permitted to spend in your company will not be forgotten by any of us.

Henry Schnitzler, California

James Willer (Carspool)
Joe Plaskett (Carbuncle)
Tom Moffat (Ptarmigan Tom)

116

Elizabeth dear: Your lake, your mountains, your tent and cabin, you made like home to us. And we shall never forget. If only we can get to visit you again!

Sally and Rockwell Kent, New York

Rice eating airport constructor.

Bill Evans, Toronto

This is the land and place of the finest and most foul weather in North America.

Ken Jones

We have been treated like kings and could not ask for a more wonderful time.

Stan Larsen & Ken Betts

Hiked in from Sunshine through sun, rain, hail and snow. Eleven hours.

Irene Reader

Ludi, Elizabeth and I with four pack-horses were the second party via Brewster's Pass — plenty of snow there and here. Caught fish nearly every day in Cerulean — three between four and five pounds.

Muriel Gratz

In 1967, Canada's centennial year, Lizzie's sisters, Jane and Nina, hiked into Sunburst Lake Camp to visit Lizzie. Jane and Nina were as tough and hardy as Lizzie; their ages of sixty-eight and sixty-six years respectively, did not deter them from making the eighteen kilometer trip.

So happy to have made it once more, so many, many thanks Lizzie.

Jane

Made it by the skin of my teeth, a centennial effort. Thousand thanks.

Geni.

CHAPTER XVII

The Parting of the Ways

THE 1967 HIKE TO SUNBURST LAKE CAMP WAS AN EFFORT FOR NINA. Only two years later she died of a stroke, on June 27, 1969, leaving Lizzie and Jane heartbroken. The three sisters who had spent sixty-eight years together on two continents, were suddenly bereft of one member. From this time onwards Jane and Lizzie leaned more and more on each other for the support that only family can give.

The following spring, still feeling the loss of their sister deeply, the two sisters joined their three long-time friends Jean Blakely, Catherine Kendal and Catherine Tosh in planning a memorial to the historic negro cowboy John Ware. A new road had been built which cut through a corner of the Fisher ranchland and separated four acres of land from the main farmland. Joe and Jane Fisher decided to donate the land for a memorial to John Ware as it was unuseable as farmland. The very pretty Ware Creek ran through these four acres and gave them a park-like appearance. John Ware had homesteaded some of the land which Elsa Basilici had originally purchased.

The five women purchased a huge rock from the rundle stone quarry at Pigeon Mountain, east of Canmore. Peter Fisher and Johnny Kendal hauled the big stone to the parcel of land, erecting it in an aesthetic manner. With the help of donations, the five ladies had a plaque made and engraved with John Ware's original brand and placed it on the stone. They invited Grant MacEwan, the Lieutenant Governor of the Province of Alberta, to dedicate the rock. MacEwan's personal interest had previously been expressed in the book "John Ware's Cow Country."

On May 30, 1970, Millarville oldtime ranchers, other interested people and invited guests (which included Ware's daughter Nettie) witnessed Grant MacEwan dedicating the monument to this historic

118

Dedication of the Ware Rock on the Fisher Ranch. Far left Nettie War. Grant Mac-Ewan, Lizzie, Jean Blakely, Jane Fisher, Catharine Tosh, Catharine Kendal.

figure. MacEwan planted a small tree on the site, as is his custom, but unfortunately, the tree later died as it was too far from the Fisher home to be watered regularly. The five ladies cooked a huge dinner for MacEwan and the invited guests, and many of the other people who attended brought lunches. Everyone joined in the festive occasion at the Fisher ranch home, the beautiful log house which Joe Fisher had built. Lizzie was proud to be part of this occasion and thrilled to meet Grant MacEwan and Nettie Ware.

Aside from the Ware rock memorial dedication, the year 1970 took on a different hue for Lizzie. This was the year in which she decided to retire from the operation of Sunburst Lake Camp. She was continually having difficulties with the provincial government and her arthritis was becoming so painful she felt it was impossible to continue the operation. Aside from these factors, she was now seventy-three years old, well past the usual retirement age. Her amazing tenacity and strength were still evident but the camp operation was becoming too strenuous.

Hundreds of memories of Sunburst Lake Camp and the Mount Assiniboine area crowded in on Lizzie as she made this decision to retire. Although her life would be changing, Lizzie could look back on almost twenty years at Sunburst Lake with deep satisfaction. Not only had there never been an accident involving her guests, but she had become steeped in the natural treasures of the area and had been a wonderful help to hundreds of hikers, skiers and climbers.

The essence of Lizzie's personality was one of the greatest drawing cards to people coming to Sunburst Lake and Mount Assiniboine. Many guests came back year after year and like Smitty Gardner, their holidays would not have been complete without a visit with Lizzie at Sunburst. After Lizzie left Sunburst Lake the essence which drew many people there was gone. While the fabulous beauty of the area remained, Lizzie's presence and unique personality left a huge hole in many hiker's lives when they returned to visit the area.

* * *

I always felt that with what I gained spiritually from the environment, from the people, from sharing with Lizzie and her friends, I should pay her.

With the people who came there, money was never discussed. The things that were discussed were things about the spirit or just enjoying one another's company. To be on a level with the person, to share what was around them, without any complications. People could talk about mountains very complicated but we had geologists and people that knew a lot about the rock who would share their knowledge in a manner that you could understand. There seemed to be an understanding between people that what was shared was shared on a level that everyone could understand. They were not people who would act as a know-it-all, or that they were the sole source of that knowledge. They shared the humbleness Lizzie also showed.

If you meet someone who is humble but also knowledgeable you put yourself on a level as Lizzie was — open. These people would open up and share without any bit of arrogance.

There were very few guests you wouldn't want to do things for or with — who wanted the service from A to Z. They wouldn't go and stay in that kind of setting if they wanted service. I think it also speaks for itself that the same kind of guests came back every year. They liked it so they came back. They came back to share that friendship again for a short time and to see Lizzie and to enjoy the mountains.

She never gave up. There were a lot of frustrations. When you have a place like that it is so hard to get people who actually want to come and work there. It is a lonely summer because it is so far away. . . . .being stuck in the wilderness unless you really like that kind of thing. . . . You can't explain the conditions I worked under because it was the whole spirit of Lizzie and the place. For me mountains meant a lot too.

So many people would ask Lizzie: "Isn't it lonely up here for you?"

"No, I've never been lonely in the mountains, never."

There is something there which is intangible. I think it has something to do with love of mountains and with love of people. She could actually bring the two together. You have climbers who love the rock and the mountain, they attach themselves to that mountain, but Lizzie could do both. She could bring the mountain to people and people to the mountain, which is what I found so magnifying. Because she loved it so much she could make others enjoy it.

Every week we had guests and the guests came back again and again, but the same rock could be just a little piece of limestone and week after week someone new would discover it and she never belittled anybody for a small discovery or a great discovery. To them she wanted it to be open so they could feel they. . . .because she was so interested in every little aspect of the environment around her, and the mountains, she noticed it and people felt she noticed it and loved it. . . .they would come to her and ask her things they might never ask anybody else. Like, do you know the name of this rock, or this flower, and she would always take time to go and look it up and find other pictures or whatever because she wanted people to actually find and enjoy it. She never attempted to teach, that wasn't her. She just wanted them to enjoy the mountains. She succeeded very well, in the people who came.

It wasn't just the mountains, it was her love of people which brought both together, which makes it a very strong tie, that those people who came back knew what they were coming to — a friendship, not only of a person but of an environment. Especially today when you see so much of the environment being destroyed by people. You wanted to keep each blade of grass in its place. Not that she was particular like that but because she had such a reverence for any living thing. This reverence gave you such a respect for everything. It is feeling those kinds of things that I could never have said no to Lizzie for another summer as long as she was going to be there. Each summer there I learned more. It was a deepening of a friendship, making the spirit stronger, but it is hard to talk about spirit.

I could say I loved working for Lizzie and I loved the mountains and it became so much a part of me, that it is still there and always will be there. Nobody can ever take it away from me, like a material good. I just learnt from that woman and from the environment, because it took both.

I don't know how you put your finger on that essence.

When you read a good book it's there. An essence that reaches the inner part of you. That really digs deeply. Being up there summers was me living a really good thing. The essence is what people bring to it as well. People are different so maybe how they relate to her and feel deeply about. . . .comes about in a different way.

There again, Lizzie had the talent of being with these different people and sharing the same essence. On a level that was enjoyment, which is a great talent. People think differently, people feel differently, their expressions are different, mentalities are so different, so that even though you have the same interests because of your mentality you cannot often relate to that person who has the same interests as you do. It is like different cultures. People are basically like that too and somehow she had the talent of bringing these people of different mentalities onto the same level to enjoy what was there.

When you work hard for something it makes a better person out of you. It is an old cliche but when you really work hard at something you enjoy doing — at the time they did these things (ranching) money wasn't available so it was work. Although she came out of the aristocracy they had to work. It's character building when you have to work for something, I think.

She was the kind of person who worked silently towards something. She hated to impose any kind of problem — she would never ask for help. Very, very independent. Probably the only reason she achieved what she did.

Today, especially when you have a little cabin, it is to get back to the land, get back to nature. People are searching for some kind of tie or link with the natural world. They feel empty somehow in the pressures of modern society. The people who came to us were not the people who were searching for their own little place, but they were people who were carrying a lot of responsibility in society as well and they needed a place where it brought out the natural sort of desires in an uncomplicated environment and in an uncomplicated manner. Just communication on a very natural, easy level and not in any way making people feel small but just to let people open up and let the pressure off their shoulders and have a good laugh or go catch a fish and just have time to look around them. This is what was so nice.

The moment she got on that horse at the end of Spray Lakes her eyes just sparkled. You could tell that that was what she had waited for all year.

She had a way of helping people as Smitty would say. I call it sharing. It's the same sort of thing. She'd put herself in anybody's shoes.

To me she was special because she could make the people feel at home and at ease with her and it's a talent very few people have. She could do this with anybody who came. I can't remember anybody who came who left in a rage such as you have at lodges, motels and hotels.

122

She had a way of making people feel good. In that sense their ego was always helped. The rock or flower or whatever. . . .she didn't tell them; she would give them a book, and she made them feel good about finding something that was beautiful in this area where she spent the whole summer. You always felt she wanted to share with you. She was there for you. She needed people too, in spite of her independence. She needed the people who would come and open up to her. She was a part of the whole thing. You see I depended on her too. In the sense that it was a job for me in the summer and. . . .sure I worked there. I did most of the physical work because it was very difficult for her to do it but I never felt that difficulty because I loved to do it. She did help me but it wasn't really help. It was something I learned — like I felt the vibrations. It was just an experience.

If you are in the area and you know Lizzie, it is like you know there is something beautiful and you want to see it. If you can you want to be able to touch something that is beautiful. That would be my feeling too now that I knew her, if I wasn't working for her and if I was in the area, it would be part of going to see her because it is something that is beautiful. When it is not a tangible thing, it is not something you can throw away. It is something you always go back to, you always enjoy it. It is hard to explain.

People need to experience this. It gives them strength. Some of the strength that she had. It never lessened her strength. It made her stronger. She was honest. You can deal with honesty because it doesn't change.

You may catch her on a day when she wasn't feeling as well — she certainly had a lot of physical pain, but that never seemed to interfere with her relationships or the conversations with people. She was smart enough to know it doesn't help to talk about yourself. You have to do something. By doing something she would either do something around the place or get involved with other people. Get involved with their ideas, their feelings and their wants and it helps you forget. If you draw back into your own sorrows and problems you don't get anywhere.

There were times at the beginning. . . .in the days at the beginning, when she would talk a little bit about her personal life, but very little. I would ask if she ever had met young men and so on. She had but she would never elaborate but because she had this potential to feel deeply I can well understand maybe she had had close relationships and they had come to an end somehow. She said during the war there were too many women for the men. It was hard to get to know anyone.

She had a bit of what her mother had as well. I only met her mother once, just before she died actually. She could go to a party and be the life of the party. She had a very special personality. She never really talked that much about her mother but she admired her very much. I think, from what she did say, that Lizzie had some of this talent her mother had for charming people. The charm that wasn't the sweet little old lady sort of thing, but she had definitely a charm that made people enjoy talking to her and being with her.

I worked for Strom one fall after I worked for Lizzie. He seemed to have a great respect for Lizzie.

Ray McBride, the outfitter, was a real character. He had that real western, packhorse, guiding. . . .expressions. . . .once watching climbers on Sunburst he said, "What are those eggs doing up there?" I can't say it like he did. Sayings. . . ."Dust on a fiddle." Ones that you hadn't heard for so long. Really neat sayings were part of his vocabulary. You really enjoyed him because he had this character.

Some of the best times were when people were there from the packhorse industry, like Ray McBride, and people from Banff, who had known Lizzie. When you get those people together you wish you had a tape recorder. When they would start talking about Jimmy Simpson and other oldtimers in the area, it was a special magic in that cabin.

I really missed the summers after Lizzie passed away. It is sad when she goes but maybe a few people will carry on that spirit she had. When people do get old there is an end to it but because she had this tremendous spirit. . . .I still have part of her in me that I learned up there and I know it's there. When I wrote to Kiwi I said that spirit still lives on because there are so many people who knew her that it just doesn't go away. The physical is dead but the spirit is still around.

I did go back into Assiniboine after Lizzie left. Herman had a climb in there. The reason I went in was because I just wanted to see Sunburst again, because Lizzie wasn't there anymore. I didn't like the idea of a youth camp being in there afterwards myself. I didn't think Lizzie liked that idea either but she didn't have much choice.

I remember going in there. They were climbing on Assiniboine. It was the end of June, first of July and there was a lot of snow still. Things don't grow back that fast there, but you could see that the environment had been abused. There was never an abuse the whole time Lizzie was there. The horses would come in and go again. They never grazed around the cabins or anything like that. There was garbage on the trees. . . .but, the government itself is not aware of these kinds of people They have these great policies and ideas but they don't know how to make them work. They knew there were maximum twelve guests in there, mostly it was ten guests and then it changed to sixteen boys, plus staff. They always complained about the environment being abused and then they come in with a helicopter every week. To me it's hypocritical.

124

Lizzie was there for nineteen summers. After I saw that I didn't want to go back again.

Lizzie's enjoyment of the land was every aspect of the whole. It was without having to alter anything. It is more beautiful if it comes up right there and you have to walk around it. This is what I found about Lizzie. It was something which didn't change. It wouldn't matter if you went back five or ten years, she would still love that little grass blade right there. She wouldn't move it.

Religion was never discussed up there, but it was present. You had respect for those living things.

Myrna (Collins) Frank

*   *   *

In late August of 1970 the last guest left Sunburst Lake and then Myrna Collins left as well. Charlie Hunter stayed on in his tent and Lizzie in her cabin until sometime in September. Although Lizzie knew there was no use looking back she did turn her head and survey the twenty years she had owned the camp and she saw they were "twenty beautiful years."

Charlie understood how much Lizzie loved Mount Assiniboine and how special the area was to her. Because he also loved the mountains, the Assiniboine area and Lizzie, he wrote her a beautiful poem to commemorate this occasion.

Slow we ride in thoughtful silence as the precious moments fly
For the summer trail is ending and the time to leave is nigh
For we've climbed our last steep summit and we've crossed our last
    divide,
Now the trail dips steeply downward winding through those stately
    trees,
Now and then our thoughts will wander on the trail to Lake Louise.

So why not let them wander . . . let them wander as they will
Mid tree-clad crags and canyons through fernclad vales and hill.

For full well we know this trail ride marks the end of golden days
As downward trail we're riding to the parting of the ways.

No more will our camp fires glimmer, birds and bees have heard the
    call
Leaves have turned from green to golden and the sunbeams slating
    fall.

Much though we love these valleys, scenic beauty is not all
For amongst life's greatest pleasures that to memory we recall,
Are those friendships made and welded mid'st the silence of the glen
That I prize far more than riches gained amongst the mark of men.

125

We have had a glorious summer beneath firs and skies azure blue
And with staunch hearts we now returneth to the tasks that men must
   do.

Much though we regret the parting with the silent shaded ways
Slaves of time we dare not linger more than our allotted days.

So take one last look across the ranges ere we bid our last adieu
Where the sunlight plays and changes and the scenes are always new
And when at last, life's journey has ended and we reached that day
   of days
May we feel the same contentment at the parting of the ways.

When Lizzie retired from Sunburst Lake, she sold the camp to the British Columbia government, who subsequently operated the camp as a boys' youth camp. Two groups of fifteen boys came for trail clearing and outdoor work, for four week periods in the summer.

And the warm glow which pervaded Sunburst Lake disappeared and only returned for fleeting moments when Lizzie went back to visit.

CHAPTER XVIII

New Adventures

IF ANY OF LIZZIE'S FRIENDS THOUGHT HER RETIREMENT FROM SUN-burst Lake was a retirement from life they were sadly mistaken.

The parttime work which Lizzie had been doing in the winters for the Archives of the Canadian Rockies in Banff continued to occupy her time. Originally, she went through old copies of the Crag and Canyon, the Banff newspaper. Eventually, Maryalice Stewart, the director of the archives at that time, wanted to interview Lizzie on a tape recorder for the archive files. Lizzie, however, would not hear of it. After much thought Mrs. Stewart succeeded in securing Lizzie as an interviewer of oldtimers. In this way Mrs. Stewart acquired some helpful information from Lizzie as well as the oldtimers who were interviewed. A most valuable asset — an oldtimer interviewing oldtimers.

In the beginning either Mrs. Stewart or Susan Davies accompanied Lizzie on the interviewing excursions. Initially Lizzie merely watched the tape recorder go round and round, but gradually she learned to ignore the machine and became involved in the conversations. Later she conducted many interviews on her own and became very adept.

Lizzie always enjoyed meeting new people, and especially young people. In 1971 she began the year managing the Eisenhower (now Castle Mountain) Youth Hostel, thirty-two kilometers west of Banff, for two weeks in January and later a week in the spring, to help the hostel manager.

Lizzie completely spoiled the hostellers.

While each hosteller is required to clean up after himself and also do a small cleaning chore, Lizzie sent the young people off skiing while she washed their dirty dishes and cleaned the hostel. It gave her

Lawrence Grassi and Lizzie at the Elizabeth Parker Hut at Lake O'Hara.

something to do she said. Lizzie was thrilled to be able to chat with the young people and also entertain her many friends who came to visit her at the hostel. It was a bit like being back at Sunburst Lake.

On June 26th Lizzie and Muriel Gratz took the bus into Lake O'Hara, just inside the British Columbia border from Alberta, and walked to the meadows above Lake O'Hara where "a small, informal but moving ceremony was held to unveil a plaque honoring Lawrence Grassi" an old and valued friend.

Lawrence Grassi, a Canmore miner, had spent approximately forty years building trails in the Lake O'Hara region and had been a friend of Lizzie's for almost as long as she had lived in the mountains. At the time of this ceremony Grassi was eighty years old and Lizzie seventy-four. The two old friends, along with a small party of devoted admirers, walked from the meadows to the Elizabeth Parker Hut (owned and operated by the Alpine Club of Canada) for tea and cake. Grassi was just as sturdy as Lizzie and possibly more so.

Grassi, although a short man, had been a phenomenally strong one in his youth. In 1925 he had accomplished an amazing feat when he walked from Canmore to Bryant Creek in one day, a distance of forty-eight kilometers; then walked to Mount Assiniboine, almost eighteen kilometers; climbed Mount Assiniboine in a solo feat the third day; hiked to the Sunshine area the fourth day, twenty-seven kilometers; and hiked from Sunshine to Banff on the fifth day, almost twenty-one kilometers. Grassi was also a prodigious climber who made a name for himself among the Banff and Lake Louise area mountaineers.

Lizzie was always extremely fond of Grassi and frequently made him delicious homemade soup during his declining years. The only thing which she did not like about him was his habit of chewing tobacco and the revolting spitoon which sat beside his favorite living room chair in his tiny home in Canmore. This idiosyncrasy of Grassi's was never allowed to interfere with their friendship. Lizzie merely ignored the habit and enjoyed Grassi for his own unique personality.

Lizzie's first summer in retirement from Sunburst Lake Camp was a very busy one as well as a very thrilling one. She did not have much time to miss the camp. Not only did she fly by helicopter into the Premier Group of mountains, west of Valemont, British Columbia, attend a luncheon at Millarville in honor of Netti Ware, and entertain her step-aunt Louisl from Germany, but she had the great thrill of flying into Mount Assiniboine with Tenzing Norgay, the man who conquered Mount Everest with Sir Edmond Hillary in 1953.

Tenzing Norgay was in Banff conducting a show in the Margaret Greenham Theatre, sponsored by the Alpine Club of Canada. Lizzie had been presented to Norgay, as a local celebrity, at a tea which was held in the Alpine Club's Clubhouse on July 13th. The following day Norgay was being flown into Mount Assiniboine to see the beautiful mountain area and Lizzie was invited to accompany him. Perfect blue

Tensing Norgay and Lizzie.

sky weather prevailed during the helicopter flight from Banff to Mount Assiniboine Provincial Park. During the flight Lizzie watched Norgay closely, wondering how he felt about her mountains. Upon receiving the first glimpse of Mount Assiniboine Lizzie turned to Norgay and said, "Of course, it is not like your mountain."

"All mountains are nice," Norgay softly answered.

Lizzie later remarked, "He was the nicest man, so humble."

This was a red letter day for Lizzie and was only marred by the fact Erling Strom was not there to share the moment with her and their illustrious guest.

Tenzing Norgay was obviously charmed by Lizzie and did not forget her. The following year Lizzie's friends Ken and Joy Williams from Missouri were in Darjeeling, India, and visited Norgay. When they told him they were friends of Lizzie Rummel's Norgay laid out the red carpet treatment, remarking he remembered Lizzie and the Calgary Stampede with great affection.

Lizzie was a very amazing person. She carried on correspondence with many people, young and old alike. Her guests from Sunburst Lake and their children often wrote to her. Smitty Gardner's son Don travelled extensively and always wrote Lizzie cards and letters. Lizzie always took an avid interest in his climbing and skiing expeditions.

Don was not the only person in whom she took an active interest. Chic Scott, Tim Auger, Lloyd Gallagher and many other young climbers were her special friends.

Many people were also interested in Lizzie as well. Periodically a newspaper or magazine would publish an article about her. Her personal charm and warmth drew people from every walk of life and the-

Lizzie, Laura and Smitty Gardner in the Kananaskis Valley.

pioneering qualities of her life had visionary appeal to many people. No one could help liking Lizzie. Many yearned to be like her. It was the pioneering qualities of Lizzie's life which inspired people to write about her and her activities.

Once Lizzie was photographed in a film entitled "Snow Foolin" in which she appeared snowshoeing in the Mount Assiniboine area.

Lizzie's age was never a barrier to stop her from doing the things she was interested in and dreamed about. She worked very hard on the Village Lake Louise project in 1972, with many of her friends, in an effort to stop the full scale expansion of the mountain park village.

Spring of 1972 saw Lizzie at Strom's lodge at Mount Assiniboine, as hostess, for the spring skiing camp in which Ruth Wilson was cook and Paul Klaas, a Swiss mountaineer, was guide. Many of her long time friends were at this camp, including Sue Davies, Pat Brewster, Sam Evans and Veijo Tiesmaki.

131

All was not well, however, with Lizzie. On July 20th she went into hospital in Calgary for twelve days to have one of her eyes removed. For some years she had had trouble with this eye after a vein had broken. Gradually she had lost her vision in the eye, although it did not bother her for several years. It eventually became inflamed and the doctor was afraid the inflamation would spread to the other eye, so she was advised to have it removed. Before the operation Lizzie was frightened she would be disfigured but afterwards, when she realized she wasn't, she became quite blasé about having an artificial eye. One time, in fact, she was in a restaurant with a friend when she looked down onto her lap and discovered her artificial eye. It had popped out. She did not get upset, but calmly put it back in the socket. Occasionally she would ask whatever friend she happened to be with, if the eye was in straight.

Og Pass. Lizzie, Charlie Hunter and Smitty Gardner.

Although Lizzie was seventy-six when she had her eye operation, she recovered from it very rapidly and was soon planning a picnic on Og Pass, near Mount Assiniboine, with some of her dearest friends. Eileen Langille was doing all Lizzie's housework for her and helping her in other ways, Charlie Hunter had cut her wood for all those years, carried water, cleaned fish and so on, and Dr. Gardner, she felt, had saved her life at least twice. The story, which is told earlier herein, unfolded at this time and stemmed from Lizzie's love for these people.

Seventy-six years old, a visit to Mount Assiniboine, an eye operation and Og Pass, but Lizzie was not through with 1973 yet. She had a dream and this was the year in which she was going to see a dream come true.

CHAPTER XIX

The Canadian Arctic

MARYALICE STEWART, LIZZIE'S FRIEND AT THE ARCHIVES IN BANFF, picked up Lizzie at her home in Canmore on September 12. Together they drove to Calgary and Smitty Gardner's home. Here Lizzie stayed overnight before leaving for the Canadian Arctic to fulfill her dream of seeing an area of which she had read prolifically. As a special treat Laura Gardner had invited her children Don and Mary Ann and Mary Ann's husband, Al, who all lived in Calgary, for dinner and a visit with Lizzie. The following morning Smitty and Laura drove Lizzie to the Calgary airport from whence she commenced her solitary journey to the North West Territories.

*   *   *

September 13th

On flight *Hay River*. Saw Great Slave Lake, start of MacKenzie River — beautiful blue. Water and lakes everywhere. *Norman Wells*, nice, mountains in distance, Mr. Wutti got out. Imperial Oil town. (Touched down here and Hay River.) Arrived *Inuvik* 3:30 p.m. — taxi eight miles to town. Eskimo Inn — supper arctic char — tour of the town. At Inuvik Airport Chris Shank came up to me. (ed. Shank was another of Lizzie's young climbing friends.) Eddy phoned 5 p.m. Phoned Ed and Valley Newcombe. He came to hotel, their home, tour of town, supper river boat.

September 14th

Walked around *Inuvik*, Indian store, library. 5 p.m. Ed Newcombe fetched me at hotel. Supper with them. Ed drove me to Shell Lake — Twin Otter float plane. Only Eskimos on board. One white woman with two babies and Eskimo husband — she told me lots. Saw *Pingos*. Tuktoyaktuk fantastic, open sea, room in guest house. Kenneth Brown. No more trees, only water. All Eskimo.

September 15th

Tuktoyaktuk — saw midnight sun at 11:30 the 14th. Got up early, sun rise, walked around. Met Eskimo, took photo of him and his boat. Bought food in Hudson's Bay store, walked to far point. Met Murray Wilson, he showed me Dr. Schwartz's artifacts. Murray has fourteen dogs and three children, boat and trapline. Left 2:55 for Inuvik. Twin Otter plane. Newcombe met me at Shell Lake wharf. Stayed in Eskimo Inn.

September 16th

Inuvik. At breakfast sat beside an Eskimo, started to talk, he was from Old Crow. Told of tragedy of yesterday where four men killed in air crash. Stephen Frost, prominent person (pilot and community person) flew on same plane as I, old D.C. Lovely flight, first Delta, myriads of little lakes, then strange formation mountains, bare hills, every which way. Then Porcupine River and Old Crow. Flew at 8,000 feet. *Old Crow* full of sadness as people close to dead man, a biologist, wives and relations of dead men all in Old Crow. District nurse at landing strip helped me carry my bags to Cooper House — good half mile. Mary Isack and husband at Cooper House. Completely modern store where I bought food. Have nice room, eat in their kitchen. House has two nice rooms for visitors. Many natives in and out, very sad. Went for walk to end of village. Log houses. Took pictures of two women with racks beside their houses with fish and meat drying. Mrs. Fanny Charlie and Mrs. Marion Nukon. Met minister had talk with him. Met woman coming towards me with good sized rail on one shoulder and piece of firewood in hand. We talked and she was Edith Josie. Shook hands and had a smoke. Was so pleased to meet Edith Josie this way. Crow Mountain in close distance; she said one hour. Made supper. Mary and Ed were out; two little girls came in and said they could do dishes. We made some toast and ate toast and jam. Soon there were more children in and out. Had good talk with Mary and Ed when they returned.

September 17th

Old Crow. Beautiful day. Walked to hospital. Herta nurse. Met Carol Feast, lovely tipi in semi-circle of trees, willows and grass. They lived there, he was on cariboo study.
People loved him and accepted him as one of them. A cariboo hide on door, spruce bow floor. Heartbreaking all his things there. Young couple, she so nice and kind.
Got lunch for Ed and Mary. One more man came on plane.

Wiring two houses. Visited Edith Josie who showed me pictures and gave me picture of herself. Is a member of Canadian Women's Press Club. They took her to Ottawa, etc. Has sore arm and spotted my bracelet, will get her one. (ed. Lizzie wore a copper bracelet for her

135

arthritis.) Supper with Ed and Mary. Met Marg Buckley (teacher) who knows Rick Kunelius.

September 18th

Old Crow. Beautiful clear and warm. Have had blister so not much walking. Met Louise Legassicke. R.C.M.P., asked in for tea, two children, only white children in school. Girl from hospital brought me pads to put on blister. Body of Dean Feast came. They are making a coffin. Two more telephone men overnight. Six little boys came in, took a picture. Children just come and go.

September 19th

Old Crow. Funeral of Dean Feast at church. They carried the coffin on big stretcher tied down with rope. Wreaths made of spruce and grasses. Impressive like all Indian ceremonies are. After lunch Neil McDonald called and talked over tea. Wish I had a tape recorder. After funeral walked to river near Cathy Netro's house. We talked and she gave me her Dad's address in Whitehorse. Took picture of her and myself. Feast in Community Hall. Carol Feast, brothers of Dean Feast. Cariboo head soup, cariboo heart, vegetables, very good. Spent evening with Ed, Mary, Sharp's, Marg Buckley. Marg gave me two Indian necklaces.

September 20th

Left *Old Crow* 10 a.m. Arrived *Whitehorse* 3:30 p.m. Beautiful flight over Ogilvie Mountains. Jean and Hank Madison came for supper at Yukon Inn. Lovely welcome. Met Cecil from Old Crow — airport maintenance man.

September 21st

Whitehorse. Overcast. Allan Innes-Taylor met me at Yukon Inn and took to his office. Very interesting, maps, talk about Yukon. Walked about town, met Innes-Taylor at 3 p.m. He took me to his house. Stayed with his wife until 5 p.m. She is a bit nutty. Jean Madison fetched me — drove to their home — wonderful supper of Arctic Char. A friend there, Mrs. Marnie Drury, friend of Jeanie's.

September 22nd

Whitehorse. Rain. To oldtimer museum, supper at Madisons. With Jeanie to Marnie Drury's for tea. Old time family business in Whitehorse.

September 23rd

Whitehorse. With Jeanie to Schwatka Lake. Miles Canyon, back over Alaska Highway to Whitehorse Indian Village. Yukon Regional Library. Gray Mountain behind house. Golden Horn south back over dam to Yukon, fish ladder. Evening with Jeanie, Hank and Syd.

September 24th

Left *Whitehorse* 9 a.m. Jeanie drove me to airport. Arrived *Inuvik*. Jan

136

Albe met me on steps of hotel. Twin Otter from Shell Lake airport to Tuktoyaktuk. American couple, Betsy and Nelson Pomeroy, Seattle. Drove to Dr. Schwartz's guest house on spit of land. Supper — cariboo stew. Visited Murray Wilson, girl there, Susan, had worked in Banff. She came up with four others in canoes to Tuktoyaktuk from Hay River. Visited at Dr. Schwartz's until 11 p.m. Pomeroys so interested too in his comments on the north. From my window I see Pingos, from toilet you look out on the Beaufort Sea. Electric heaters and a fireplace. Cariboo skins for rugs. Dr. Schwartz lent me rubber boots.

September 25th

Tuktoyaktuk. Beautiful sunrise. Walked to end of spit, put my feet in Beaufort Sea! Lunch with Pomeroys in cabin. 3 p.m. with Murray Wilson in his small boat. Rusty Lister engine — out to sea and around island where dogs are kept. Met huge tugboat going into big waves. Lots of seagulls, past DEW line installation. After supper over to Murray's. Dr. Schwartz came over. The doctor a queer man, bit of a humbug. Jewish people not too fond of him. Asked carpenter for supper. Nice man from New Brunswick — gets $1,000 a month, works 15 hours a day. Natives all so friendly, talked to many. Lovely sunset.

September 26th

Tuktoyaktuk. Walked to village and Hudson's Bay fur shop. Bought caps and slippers for Bims. Esther Courtney in fur shop, mother-in-law of Linda Courtney. Twin Otter from Tuk to Inuvik, from Shell airport to big airport just half hour. Ed and Vally Newcombe at airport. To Yellowknife — lovely flight — Yellowknife Inn.

September 27th

Yellowknife. Mrs. M. E. Braathen (travel counsellor), old time family in Yellowknife: pre-Cambrian rock formation from Norman Wells to Yellowknife. Going south — Franklin Mountains on left, McKenzie Mountains on right. Mrs. B. drove me to bush pilot monument overlooking old town, Great Slave Lake, explained where first settlers settled on Latham Island. Drove me around town. 5 p.m. to airport on standby. 7:15 left for *Calgary*: arrived Calgary 9:35 p.m. Bims, Jody, Jim, Smitty, Jim and Deirdre Willer at airport. Had a little visit with Willers then drove home to Bims'.
End of a wonderful fifteen days.

Lizzie's diary.

*   *   *

Because Lizzie had so many friends in so many different places, it is impossible to explain or to know who she previously knew before going on this arctic trip. It is certain, however, she knew Jean and Hank Madison and Ed and Valerie Newcombe.

Lizzie made friends wherever she went. Hers was the unique personality. She could walk down a street in a strange village and make five friends in one block. Going to Old Crow, Inuvik and Tuktoyaktuk and making friends with everyone she met, being invited on a boat trip, or for tea, or to share a smoke was all part of Lizzie's charisma.

Lizzie made two trips to Tuktoyaktuk because she had previously arranged her flights from one place to another. When she first went to Tuktoyaktuk she had no idea what to expect and was so pleased with the village and the people she met, she immediately wanted to return.

Lizzie's Canadian Arctic adventure was a dream which she had had for a long, long time. Realizing the dream, although seventy-six years old, was a special joy and accomplishment. What were a few blisters to the joy of meeting so many interesting people and seeing this land which was so fascinating to her?

Picture a short, squarely built woman with a crop of beautiful white, curly hair, walking gingerly along a dirt street, a cane in one hand, peering at the Inuit women drying meat and fish outside their small homes, and Inuit women just as curious to see this lone, elderly woman in this out-of-the-way place. All things put together, the two quite naturally were of interest to each other.

An old man with a boat, sitting on the edge of the Beaufort Sea, high in the arctic tundra, looking off the edge of the world, turns and sees this same white-haired woman approaching. The look in her eyes is not that of an old person but a look of lively, active interest. At once the old man is drawn to her and together they share the joy of riding on the waters at the top of the world. A unique thrill to the white-haired lady and to the old man a deep pleasure to find someone who loves the land and sea as he does.

CHAPTER XX

More Stories

LIZZIE HAD DONE MOST OF HER TRAVELLING AS A YOUNG GIRL although she was seventy-six when she went to the Canadian Arctic, but her friend Charlie Hunter did most of his travelling as an old man. Charlie went looking for adventure at the age of seventy-four in South America, where he spent three months looking at Inca ruins, walking in the High Andes, travelling in the upper reaches of the Amazon River, viewing the Pampas of Argentina and the lake country of Chile, as well as visiting most of the South American capitals, Australia and Mount Cook in New Zealand. Charlie also spent eight months in Africa travelling from Cape Town to the Suez Canal and, at seventy-eight years, travelled to the Orient where he bought a motor bike. Charlie never went as a tourist, but as a traveller, hence a motor bike was more to his liking.

Charlie was eighty-four years old the year he showed up in Oslo, Norway, looking for Erling Strom who had retired to his homeland. In a tourist information kiosk Charlie was trying to communicate he was looking for Strom, but he was having difficulties as he not only could not speak Norwegian, but he could no longer hear. Everything had to be written down. Eventually, the girl in the kiosk came to understand what Charlie wanted and telephoned Strom: "Did he know a man from Canada who could not hear?" Strom immediately knew about whom the girl was speaking and arrangements were made to see Charlie.

During the course of Charlie's visit with Strom, Charlie said, "I sure like Norway. I am going to move and live here when I get old."

*   *   *

"You must spend a terrible lot of money travelling Charlie. . . ."

"I do. I have worked hard all my life to earn it, and I hope to live long enough to use it up. I can't take it with me."

Dr. J. S. Gardner

Charlie died in 1982 at the age of ninety-four. . . . we hope he used it up before he went.

Like Charlie, it would be impossible for Lizzie to retire in the true sense of the word. It was quite against her nature. She seemed to be as busy as ever in spite of retiring from Sunburst Camp. People came to visit her at her home in Canmore; she spent countless hours working in her garden, which was one of the prettiest in Canmore; and things kept happening to her.

The dedication of Mount Jimmy Simpson took place on August 8, 1975, at Num-ti-jah Lodge, forty-eight kilometers north of Lake Louise, on the shore of Bow Lake. Lizzie attended the ceremony and the luncheon, visiting with old friends. Tom Parkin, of Castlegar, British Columbia, wrote Lizzie asking for help in compiling a checklist of birds in Mount Assiniboine Provincial Park. Lizzie had a great love for birdlife and was very willing to help. Ray Legace, Lizzie's Skoki outfitter, died and Lizzie tried her best to console Alpha, his wife. Alpha had spent many years working hard running the Post Hotel in Lake Louise while Ray outfitted for Lizzie and others. Ray was "a character who should be in Dickens Pickwick Papers" and was "the strangest, lovingest, silliest old person that ever lived."

Also, Peter Saunders, Lizzie's cousin from Scotland (son of Traudl Soloschin) visited Lizzie, as well as spending a week skiing at Hans Gmoser's Bugaboo Lodge in the Purcell Mountains of British Columbia. Someone from the Toronto newspaper, The Globe and Mail, interviewed Lizzie and ran an article in their weekend magazine.

> One of the things dear to her heart was the meeting of minds
> and fascinating conversation around the campfire at night.
> Too many people would spoil the magic of those moments.

There was no end to the swirl of activity in Lizzie's life and that was just the way she wanted to live.

As well as activity, there was also a lot of pain in Lizzie's life. She once said she had never known a day without pain for over twenty years. That twenty years eventually added up to thirty years.

At the age of seventy-eight Lizzie once more was admitted to hospital in Calgary. This time to have a hip joint replacement in her other hip, due to the dreadful arthritis which was creeping slowly but surely throughout her body. Unfortunately, she spent another Christmas in hospital.

*   *   *

I had to describe it in detail; tell her about the dozens of people; tell her about the anaesthetic (how it clears old folks lungs out now).

I went over to see her the night before the operation and she said, "Now I want your undivided attention without any argument."

"What the hell, I never argue with you."

"You always argue with me. You know how many chances there are for me to die with this operation."

"Yes, there are about that — zero."

"You make fun of it, but that's because you are a doctor."

"You, Lizzie, darling, we. . . .I can't be more serious."

"That's it. I think I'm going to die and you don't and if I'm going to die there is one thing I want before I die. . . .I want you to have this, so please take it and shut up."

What the object was is confidential. I can't tell you.

Dr. J. S. Gardner

*   *   *

Lizzie didn't die as she supposed. She was up and walking around within a couple of days after the operation and extremely pleased she had such tremendous relief from the terrible pain. It was not long before Lizzie was home and back in harness; filling her calendar with activities.

The following year the Millarville Dance Hall was donated to Heritage Park in Calgary. The hall had been built on Joe and Jane Fisher's ranchland where, for many years, it was the scene of dances, weddings and other community events. Lizzie, Jane and Nina had spent many hours dancing in the hall and it held precious memories. Heritage Park held a special ceremony in 1976 in honor of achieving this historic hall for their display. Lizzie attended the Millarville Day Celebration at Heritage Park as hostess and guest.

From the Millarville dance hall Lizzie could look across the park lawns and see the little curling cabin in which she had lived beside the Bow River in Banff.

Lizzie had the joy of flying in a Bell 214 helicopter when she was eighty years old. She went from Banff, to Golden, British Columbia, north to the Cariboo Mountains and landed at Hans Gmoser's Cariboo Lodge where she lunched with Gmoser, Lloyd Gallagher and other friends. From the lodge the party flew to Victor Glacier and Victor Lake, twice setting down on little pinacles where they were able to get out and walk around. Lizzie found the experience intoxicating and gratifying — seeing "terrific glaciers."

Lizzie made another flight into Mount Assiniboine in September and visited Sunburst Lodge with the Banff pilot Jim Davies and his wife Sue. Lizzie found great delight in being able to sit around the table in her former cabin, drinking tea and making new friends of Kieron and Eva, the ranger and his wife.

Lizzie at her home in Canmore.

Lizzie found there was always something to do or someone visiting her. One gorgeous spring day Jean Gill drove to Canmore from Calgary and took Lizzie to Lake louise and Bow Lake. At Bow Lake Lizzie had a long visit with young Jim Simpson. On the ride home, however, she was so stiff she rode in the back seat of the car where she could stretch out. Upon their arrival at her home in Canmore, Jean had to literally pull Lizzie out of the car by the shoulders. She just couldn't move her arthritis had stiffened her up so much, but she said it was worth it.

One of Lizzie's most admirable qualities was her determination not to give up living a full and active life in spite of her deteriorating arthritis. Not long after her hip joint replacement the arthritis moved into her spine and became more and more painful. She would not, however, give in but continued to be busy.

What does a lady of eighty-one years do with her time? Some are

142

ill, some are lonely, some sit in senior citizens' lodges or nursing homes waiting for a visitor. . . . and then there is Lizzie.

In Lizzie's eighty-first year she had four hundred and sixty-four recorded visitors, went out to dinner sixty-four times, went to thirty-five plays or slide shows, made two trips into Mount Assiniboine of nine days total, and spent twenty days, in two visits, in hospital. This did not include her many visits to Calgary, by bus, to visit her sister Jane who was in hospital with a broken hip; nor her visit to Kananaskis Provincial Park for the grand opening of the park, which was opened by the premier of Alberta, Peter Lougheed. On this latter occasion Lizzie met again after many years, Norma Pocaterra the widow of George Pocaterra, of Kananaskis fame.* Lizzie and Mrs. Pocaterra had known each other during Lizzie's years on the Millarville ranch.

Truly Lizzie was an amazing woman.

*The Valley of Rumours. . . .the Kananaskis, by the author.

CHAPTER XXI

The Order of Canada

LIZZIE WAS SUCH A REMARKABLE WOMAN IN HER ACHIEVEMENTS IN helping people relate to the mountain environment, and so endearing on a personal level to many people, that a number of her very close and influential friends recommended she receive The Order of Canada award. Lizzie was unaware of their efforts. The first time she heard of the award was on December 20, 1979, when she received notification she was to receive The Order of Canada and the Canada Medal. Lizzie was completely stunned at the announcement and immediately telephoned Smitty Gardner.

"There has been a terrible mistake."

Lizzie was sure the officials had the wrong person.

"No, there is no mistake," Smitty said.

Lizzie recovered from the shock of this announcement in due course and then made plans to be in Ottawa for the presentation of The Order of Canada which was to take place on April 16, 1980. Fortunately, Liana Van Der Bellen, who had worked for Lizzie many years before at Sunburst Camp, was living in Ottawa as she was now working in the Parliamentary Library. Liana invited Lizzie to stay with her while attending the investiture.

Lizzie was not feeling very well at this time, but she made the journey to Ottawa anyway. Wearing the elegant, black dress which her father had given to her thirty years before, Elizabeth von Rummel accepted the Canada Medal from Governor General Edward Schreyer. In this beautiful dress, which knew no age in its style, Lizzie did look like the Baroness Elisabet von Rummel.

The Order of Canada citation read:

Mountaineer *par excellence*, protector of the environment, authority on local flora and fauna, and friend to countless

144

Elizabeth Rummel receiving the Order of Canada from Governor General Edward Schreyer. Mrs. Schreyer on the right and Liana Van Der Bellen on the left.

hikers in the mountains near Banff. She has enriched her country by sharing her deep love of the Rocky Mountains with all who meet her.

To Canada, this mountain lady had fulfilled the requirements The Order of Canada had been created to honor.

. . . .created to recognize outstanding achievement and service in most fields of human endeavour.

To many people Lizzie was also the baroness of the Canadian Rocky Mountains because of her caring for and sharing of these mountains.

Less than a month after the Canadian award, Lizzie was named the First Lady of the Town of Canmore by the Canmore Sigma Phi. On May 9, 1980, at a Mothers' Day luncheon in the Union Hall in Canmore, the award was presented by Edna Appleby the first lady of the previous year.

Lizzie had been active in the Canmore Library since 1971. Initially, she had worked with Mildred Fisher, Claire Storey and Stan Dowhan on the first library board, in setting up the library. The library was first in a room in the town's firehall, it now reposes in a beautiful building with over twelve thousand volumes and nine hundred members. Lizzie and her friend Joyce Cole had cut the ribbon for the new library on January 12, 1980. Lizzie remained a member of the library board until her death.

The presentation of the First Lady of the Year award was one of the ways in which the Town of Canmore showed their appreciation to Lizzie for her efforts in the community and library development.

Lizzie's life was drawing to a close, but it was hard to tell. Not only was 1980 the year she received The Order of Canada, but she was busy in other ways as well. On February 16th she had attended, by special invitation, the dedication of the new Sunshine Village Gondola. Her old friend "Jackrabbit" Smith-Johannsen was the dedicator of the new gondola and Lizzie enjoyed meeting him again.

Lizzie also continued to receive many letters from her friends around the world. One day she received a letter from Edwin Grimm of Wadenswil, Switzerland, a man who had visited Sunburst Lake in 1954.

I met you down at the little lake and I said: "It's absolutely fantastic here," and you said, "Sie meinen fantastisch, ja das werde ich Ihnen nie vergessen."

Grimm had been very surprised to hear his native tongue spoken in that far-off wilderness resort. It was a surprise which he still remembered almost thirty years later and wrote to Lizzie about. Grimm was only one of hundreds of people who remembered Lizzie and her lake.

In June Hans Gmoser had a special party at his Bugaboo Lodge in the Purcell Mountains of British Columbia. He invited his very old friends, particularly the first friends he had when he came to Canada from Austria. People who had done a lot for him. Of course, Lizzie was invited, because it was important to Gmoser Lizzie be there. Lizzie went to the party although she was not feeling at all well.

*   *   *

So we picked her up and drove her up there. Such a lovely affair. Such a nice place and the weather was beautiful. Lizzie enjoyed it so much. . . . seeing many people she had known before. She was so sick then I didn't know how she could stand it. She would smile and laugh and talk. She would eat a little wee bit. She looked so badly. I thought, Lizzie must have cancer of the stomach. We had a friend the same way. Every time we saw her in the summer she would look worse. She looked so sick. The whole summer went by and nothing was done, although they were doing tests and things. I knew darn well what was the matter with her. Yet when they operated it was so far advanced.

That day or so up at the Bugaboos, she just had a lovely time. We

146

stayed in a place at Fairmont and Lizzie had a little room off ours and she slept soundly all night long.

Laura Gardner

*　　*　　*

As the summer wore on Lizzie became more and more ill and the doctors seemed to be more and more baffled. She had taken anti-inflamatory drugs for her arthritis for so many years it was thought she had an ulcer. A common consequence.

Then, on the first of July Lizzie was shocked and upset to receive the news her great nephew, Jim Fisher, had been killed in an auto accident near Millarville. Lizzie had always doted on her three nephews and was equally devoted to all of their children. Jimmy's death was a great blow to her, as well as to the whole family. Jane, Jimmy's grandmother, never fully recovered from the shock. The shock of Jimmy's death undermined Lizzie's struggle with illness. Her health continued to deteriorate and, like Laura Gardner, many of Lizzie's friends were very worried.

Lizzie was admitted to the Foothills Hospital in Calgary at the end of the summer. After being observed for several days she was operated on in early September.

*　　*　　*

I felt much better about her when she was in the hospital and she was being looked after and being given something for the pain. She seemed to lose this strained expression she had had all the time during the summer. Ella Mae felt a lot better about her too.

Laura Gardner

*　　*　　*

When we opened her up she was just full of what we call carcinomatosis. It is a spread of abdominal cancer which just spreads everywhere. . . .sort of what we call seeding. Little patches of it. Small tumors all through. There is nothing you can do about it. It is just so much you have to take the whole abdomen out. We just closed her up.

People with that much abdomen and that much cancer burst open easier, especially older people, so we had to sew her up quite tightly and when they sew up that tightly it hurts like the mischief. She wanted me to cut the stitches but I couldn't cut the stitches in case she would burst open. Until that pain stopped she was really suffering a lot, but as soon as the swelling went down and they took the stitches out her pain wasn't all that bad and she didn't need nearly as much medicine. She was hallucinating a little when taking all that medicine.

One day she said to me, "Do you think I could ever get back to Canmore?"

"Yeah, when?"

"I could?"

"How about tomorrow?"

"You wouldn't tease me now?"

"Sure I would. Why wouldn't I tease you now.?"

"Well, I'm going to die."

"Damn it, I'll tease you 'til you die."

She had been told at that stage it would kill her. The surgeon didn't tell her in so many words so I explained the whole thing to her. She said, "Well, I didn't want to die of cancer."

"Don't be like Mother. It isn't any fault of anybody. (Mother always thought it was somebody's fault.) Don't be that way. Everybody dies of cancer eventually; what the hell."

"I could have had a heart attack or a stroke."

"No, no, this is the way it is."

"Well, I've had a good life, haven't I?"

"Yeah, you sure as hell have since I met you."

"I just worry about Janey."

"Look, Janey is made of the kind of stuff that you're made of."

"What do you mean?"

"You do best against adversity. You're best when it's uphill. You're not a downhill person."

"Do you think she'll be better without me?"

"She won't be better but she will be alright."

"Oh, you're just saying that."

"No, I'm not. Damn it, I'm a doctor."

"Oh, I guess you are a doctor."

"Sure, Janey will be stronger when she needs to be."

"Do you really believe that?"

"Of course I believe it, or I wouldn't say it."

"Who will look after her?"

"There is always somebody else, there is another guy around the corner to do what we've been doing when we're gone. It's been going on that way for years."

"Well, that's the only worry I have."

"Don't you worry about yourself?"

"Not a bit. I'm eighty-three, who wants to live much longer?"

"I don't know. You've had quite a life."

"Yes I have. I don't want to leave my friends. The only problem is Janey."

She wanted to say to me will you look after her. She never did. I did impress upon her that Janey is the kind of person she is.

When I went to see her the first time after she was moved to Canmore Hospital she said, "Can you see the trees, and the leaves?"

"Yeah, Chinaman's Peak is out there."

"Thank you, thank you."

She said once or twice to me. "Too many visitors."

"Yeah, you know, they just want to be with you. Don't talk to them."

"I have to talk."

She loved seeing people.

Dr. J. S. Gardner

*   *   *

As the days wore on, Lizzie became weaker and weaker and could speak less and less. Her sister Jane visited her every day and stayed by her side as long as possible and many of her friends and other relatives also visited her daily.

*   *   *

The day I went to see Lizzie at Canmore Hospital she was sleeping and had had a lot of visitors, so I didn't wake her; I just went away planning to go back again. By chance I was asked to run the Alpine Club Clubhouse, just outside of Canmore, the next week. When I was there I would go over to the hospital every day to see her, but each time I went she either had too many visitors or was sleeping after having too many visitors. I didn't want to wear her out so I would go away without seeing her.

On the Thursday morning I had a strong feeling I should go and see her that morning. After helping a fellow get his truck battery to a garage I went to the hospital. Of course, it was morning so she did not have visitors, although she was sleeping, probably due to the heavy drugs she was being given. The nurse woke her up by brushing her forehead and talking to her. She looked up at me without saying a word. I held her hand and brushed her forehead and as I gazed down at her I realized the cancer and impending death were beginning to make her look ugly and discolored, but suddenly I was overwhelmed with such a surge of totally uninhibited love for her I instinctively bent my head over her and whispered, "I love you Lizzie."

She smiled, but didn't open her eyes.

I realized then she couldn't talk anymore but she could still hear, so I continued brushing her forehead, and then, just as suddenly, and without thinking, I blurted out: "Say hello to Jesus for me when you get there."

After that there really wasn't much more to say. I only stayed a few more minutes before saying goodbye and turning to leave. As I reached the foot of her bed I looked back and she was looking directly at me with her eyes as big as saucers. I couldn't even tell which eye was the artificial one. I waved goodbye and was gone.

Ruthie

*   *   *

Within two hours Lizzie slipped into a coma and never regained consciousness. The next evening, Friday, October 10, 1980, she quietly stopped breathing.

Janey, Lizzie's sister, was with her every day while she was in hospital, both in Calgary and Canmore.

I did everything I possibly could for her. I couldn't have done more.

Nor could anyone else.

*   *   *

We just didn't think Lizzie would die. I don't think anybody thought she would. It just seemed to me that Lizzie was here and would be.

Laura Gardner

*   *   *

Lizzie's body was sent to the University of Calgary, according to her wishes, but the university could not use it for their research purposes. It was sent to Banff and cremated.

A memorial service was held for Lizzie on October 14th, at the Jacques Funeral Home in Banff.

Lizzie did not attend.

Lizzie was off on a new and more exciting adventure.

Epilogue

"Recently, Hans Gmoser of Banff has offered a second scholarship to provide financial assistance to aspirant guides. This scholarship is to be known as the Lizzie Rummel Memorial Scholarship, and honors the memory of Elizabeth Rummel who passed away in October, 1980, in Canmore. The committee administering the Wolodarsky Scholarship will also be responsible for the Rummel Scholarship."

The Gazette
Published by The Alpine
Club of Canada
May 1981

*   *   *

High on Mount Galatea a small lake is situated from whence flows a creek into the Spray Lakes Reservoir which is located a short distance west of the Town of Canmore. In the autumn of 1983 the administrative offices of the Kananaskis Country recreation area approved the naming of this lake and creek to be Rummel Lake and Rummel Creek. The naming of the lake and creek has been presented to the Alberta Provincial Government for their approval. Final naming approval comes from the federal government offices in Ottawa. We trust Rummel Lake and Rummel Creek are an official reality as you read these words.

R.O.

*   *   *

Bibliography

Alpine Club of Canada camp register 1942, Alpine Club of Canada Archives, Archives of the Canadian Rockies, Banff.

Auger, Timothy, personal communication 1981.

Bagley, James, personal communication 1981.

Baptie, Robert tape interview, 1971 Archives of the Canadian Rockies, Banff.

Arnes, Jenny, Barnes, George (Barney), McGowan, Bill, Rummel, Lizzie, tape interview 1970, Archives of the Canadian Rockies, Banff.

Boles, Glen W., Kruszyna, Robert and Putnam, William L., Climbers Guide to the Rocky Mountains of Canada South. Banff: American Alpine Club and Canadian Alpine Club, 1979.

Boyce, James, tape interview 1971, Archives of the Canadian Rockies, Banff.

Boyce, James and Dorothy, personal communication 1981.

Brewster, F. O., papers, Archives of the Canadian Rockies, Banff.

Brewster, F. O. "Pat," Weathered Wood, Banff 1977.

Brigden, Arnold, letters, E. Rummel collection, Archives of the Canadian Rockies, Banff.

Brunn, Geoffrey, The World in the Twentieth Century. Boston: Heath and Company, 1957.

Calgary Herald, The, December 9, 1971, p. 26.

Calhoun, Alex, tape interview 1971, Archives of the Canadian Rockies, Banff.

Chalmers, Jackie, Western Stockgrowers Association newsletter, Vol. III, No. 10, October 1978, member of the month.

Cockerton, D., Lake Louise land use history, background paper for Lake Louise development planning process. Parks Canada 1978.

Conway, Mary, Canadian Alpine Journal, June 1948, Vol. XXXI, "Glacier Camp" July 1947.

DeBrul, Fr. Peter, personal communication 1981.

Deegan, James, personal communication 1980.

Deegan, Jim and Porter, John, Timberline Tales. Banff: The Peter Whyte Foundation, 1977.

Fairless, Wilf, tape interview 1970, Archives of the Canadian Rockies, Banff.

Fisher, Jane, personal communications 1980/81.

152

Frank, Myrna, personal communication 1981.

Fraser, Esther, The Canadian Rockies, Early travels and explorations. Edmonton: Hurtig, 1969.

Fraser, Esther, Wheeler. Banff: Summerthought, 1978.

Fuller, Jack and Cyril, tape interview 1969, Archives of the Canadian Rockies, Banff.

Fulmer, A. G., article on Banff library and archives, 1968, Archives of the Canadian Rockies, Banff.

Gallagher, Lloyd, personal communication 1981.

Gardner, Dr. J. S. and Laura, personal communication 1981.

Gazette, The, Number 97, May 1981. Ottawa: Alpine Club of Canada.

Gest, Lillian, History of Mount Assiniboine, 1979.

Gill, Jean, personal communication 1981.

Grassi, Lawrence and Jones, Ken, tape interview 1971, Archives of the Canadian Rockies, Banff.

Gratz, Muriel, personal communication 1980.

Harmon, Aileen, personal communication 1980.

Harris, Lawren and Bess, Christmas card 1968, E. Rummel collection, Archives of the Canadian Rockies, Banff.

Harrison, Bill, tape interview 1976, Archives of the Canadian Rockies, Banff.

Hart, E. J., Diamond Hitch, The early outfitters of Banff and Jasper. Banff: Summerthought, 1979.

Horspool, Mrs., tape interview 1970, Archives of the Canadian Rockies, Banff.

Hunter, Charlie, tape interview 1969, Archives of the Canadian Rockies, Banff.

Hunter, Charles, personal communication 1981.

Jones, Kenneth and Bridget, personal communication 1981.

Kicking Horse News, August and September 1964, Archives of the Canadian Rockies, Banff.

LaCasse, Annie and Ulus, tape interview 1970, Archives of The Canadian Rockies, Banff.

Lamarque, Ernest C. W., E. Rummel collection, Archives of the Canadian Rockies, Banff.

Langille, Eileen, personal communication 1980.

Luxton, Eleanor G., Banff, Canada's first national park. Banff: Summerthought, 1975.

McDowell, Catharine, personal communication 1981.

Mosel, Tad with Macey, Gertrude, Leading Lady, The world and theatre of Katharine Cornell. Boston, Toronto: Little Brown & Company, 1978.

Munday, Phylis, tape interview 1972, Archives of the Canadian Rockies, Banff.

Our Foothills, Millarville, Kew, Priddis and Bragg Creek Historical Society, 1975.

Paris, Cyril, tape interview 1970, Archives of the Canadian Rockies, Banff.

Patton, Brian and Robinson, Bart, The Canadian Rockies trail guide. Canmore: Devil's Head Press, 1978.

Pendergast, Bert, tape interview 1977, Archives of the Canadian Rockies, Banff.

Plaskett, Joseph, personal communication 1981.

For Rainy Days at Mt. Assiniboine 1962, scrapbook, E. Rummel collection, Archives of the Canadian Rockies, Banff.

Roberts, Mrs. Dick, tape interview 1972, Archives of the Canadian Rockies, Banff.

Rummel, Elizabeth, tape interview 1976, Archives of the Canadian Rockies, Banff.

Ski Bulletin, The, December 1940, Vol. XI, No. 4.

Skoki Lodge file, May 1965, Archives of the Canadian Rockies, Banff.

Skoki Lodge guest registers, 1943 to 1947, Archives of the Canadian Rockies, Banff.

Stavrianos, Leften S. and others, A global history of man. Boston: Allyn & Bacon, 1970.

Stewart, Maryalice, personal communication 1981.

Strom, Erling, tape interview, Archives of the Canadian Rockies, Banff.

Strom, Erling, Pioneers on Skis. Central Valley, New York: Smith Clove Press, 1977.

Strom, Erling, personal communications 1981.

Strom, Siri, tape interview, Archives of the Canadian Rockies, Banff.

Taylor, William C., The snows of yesteryear, J. Norman Collie Mountaineer. Toronto, Montreal: Holt, Rinehart and Winston of Canada, 1973.

Vallance, Peter, personal communication 1981.

Vallance, S. R., Lawrence Grassi, Canadian Alpine Journal 1977.

Vallance, Sydney, tape interview, Archives of the Canadian Rockies, Banff.

Vernon-Wood-Sattmann, Ruth, tape interview 1976, Archives of the Canadian Rockies, Banff.

Walls, Jean, personal communication 1981.

Watson, Sir Norman J., Skiing development in North America, June 1937, Archives of the Canadian Rockies, Banff.

Wells, H. G., The outline of history Volume 2. New York: Doubleday, 1971.

Whyte, Catharine, personal papers 1948, Archives of the Canadian Rockies, Banff.

Whyte, Jon, personal communications 1980/81.

Willer, James and Deidre, personal communication 1981.

Wright, Bill, tape interview 1970, Archives of the Canadian Rockies, Banff.

Zeman, Z. A. B., Twilight of the Hapsburgs. London: St. Giles House, 1971.

*   *   *